JACKIE ROBINSON

OVERCOMING ADVERSITY

JACKIE ROBINSON

Gina De Angelis

Introduction by James Scott Brady,
Trustee, the Center to Prevent Handgun Violence
Vice Chairman, the Brain Injury Foundation

Chelsea House Publishers
Philadelphia

The Author Wishes to Dedicate This Book to Therese De Angelis.

Cover photos: UPI/Corbis-Bettman

CHELSEA HOUSE PUBLISHERS

PRODUCTION MANAGER Pamela Loos
ART DIRECTOR Sara Davis
DIRECTOR OF PHOTOGRAPHY Judy L. Hasday
MANAGING EDITOR James D. Gallagher
SENIOR PRODUCTION EDITOR J. Christopher Higgins

Staff for **JACKIE ROBINSON**
PROJECT EDITOR Rob Quinn
ASSOCIATE ART DIRECTOR/DESIGNER Takeshi Takahashi
PICTURE RESEARCHER Patricia Burns
COVER DESIGNER Keith Trego

The Chelsea House World Wide Web site address is:
http://www.chelseahouse.com

First Printing

1 3 5 7 9 8 6 4 2

Library of Congress Cataloging-in-Publication Data

De Angelis, Gina.
Jackie Robinson / Gina De Angelis; introduction by James Scott Brady.
  p. cm. — (Overcoming adversity)
Includes bibliographical references and index.

ISBN 0-7910-5897-2 — ISBN 0-7910-5898-0 (pbk.)

1. Robinson, Jackie, 1919–1972—Juvenile literature. 2. Baseball players—United
States— Biography— Juvenile literature. 3. Afro-American baseball players—
Biography— Juvenile literature. [1. Robinson, Jackie 1919–1972. 2. Baseball players.
3. Afro-Americans—Biography.] I. Title. II. Series.

GV865.R6 D42 2000
7966.357'092—dc21
[B]
                                                        00-043200

CONTENTS

ON FACING ADVERSITY *James Scott Brady*   7

1 WHEN THE FIGHT WAS JUST BEGINNING   11

2 AN OFFICER AND A SHORTSTOP   21

3 A MONARCH AND A ROYAL   33

4 JACKIE PUTS A FOOT IN THE DOOR   47

5 PUSHING THE DOOR WIDE OPEN   57

6 STEALING HOME   67

7 THE LAST INNINGS   81

CHRONOLOGY   94

JACKIE ROBINSON'S STATISTICS   96

FURTHER READING   98

INDEX   100

OVERCOMING ADVERSITY

TIM ALLEN
comedian/performer

MAYA ANGELOU
author

THE APOLLO 13 MISSION
astronauts

LANCE ARMSTRONG
professional cyclist

DREW BARRYMORE
actress

DREW CAREY
comedian/performer

JIM CARREY
comedian/performer

BILL CLINTON
U.S. president

TOM CRUISE
actor

MICHAEL J. FOX
actor

WHOOPI GOLDBERG
comedian/performer

EKATERINA GORDEEVA
figure skater

SCOTT HAMILTON
figure skater

JEWEL
singer and poet

JAMES EARL JONES
actor

QUINCY JONES
musician and producer

ABRAHAM LINCOLN
U.S. president

WILLIAM PENN
Pennsylvania's founder

JACKIE ROBINSON
baseball legend

ROSEANNE
entertainer

MONICA SELES
tennis star

SAMMY SOSA
baseball star

DAVE THOMAS
entrepreneur

SHANIA TWAIN
entertainer

ROBIN WILLIAMS
performer

BRUCE WILLIS
actor

STEVIE WONDER
entertainer

ON FACING ADVERSITY

James Scott Brady

I GUESS IT'S a long way from a Centralia, Illinois, train yard to the George Washington University Hospital Trauma Unit. My dad was a yardmaster for the old Chicago, Burlington & Quincy Railroad. As a child, I used to get to sit in the engineer's lap and imagine what it was like to drive that train. I guess I always have liked being in the "driver's seat."

Years later, however, my interest turned from driving trains to driving campaigns. In 1979, former Texas governor John Connally hired me as a press secretary in his campaign for the American presidency. We lost the Republican primary to a former Hollywood star named Ronald Reagan. But I managed to jump over to the Reagan campaign. When Reagan was elected in 1980, I was "sitting in the catbird seat," as humorist James Thurber would say—poised to be named presidential press secretary. I held that title throughout the eight years of the Reagan administration. But not without one terrible, extended interruption.

It happened barely two months after the Reagan administration took office. I never even heard the shots. On March 30, 1981, my life went blank in an instant. In an attempt to assassinate President Reagan, John Hinckley Jr. armed himself with a "Saturday night special"—a low-quality, $29 pistol—and shot wildly as our presidential entourage exited a Washington hotel. One of the exploding bullets struck me just above the left eye. It shattered into a couple dozen fragments, some of which penetrated my skull and entered my brain.

The next few months of my life were a nightmare of repeated surgery, broken contact with the outside world, and a variety of medical complications. More than once, I was very close to death.

The next few years were filled with frustrating struggles to function with a paralyzed right side, struggles to speak and communicate.

To people who face and defeat daunting obstacles, "ambition" is not becoming wealthy or famous or winning elections or awards. Words like "ambition" and "achievement" and "success" take on very different meanings. The objective is just to live, to wake up every morning. The goals are not lofty; they are very ordinary.

My own heroes are ordinary folks—but they accomplish extraordinary things because they try. My greatest hero is my wife, Sarah. She's accomplished a lot of things in life, but two stand out. The first has been the way she has cared for me and our son since I was shot. A tremendous tragedy and burden was dropped unexpectedly into her life, totally beyond her control and without justification. She could have given up; instead, she focused her energies on preserving our family and returning our lives to normal as much as possible. Week by week, month by month, year by year, she has not reached for the miraculous, just for the normal. Yet in focusing on the normal, she has helped accomplish the miraculous.

Her other most remarkable accomplishment, to me, has been spearheading the effort to keep guns out of the hands of criminals and children in America. Opponents call her a "gun grabber"; I call her a national hero. And I am not alone.

After a seven-year battle, during which Sarah and I worked tirelessly to educate the public about the need for stronger gun laws, the Brady Bill became law in 1993. It was a victory, achieved in the face of tremendous opposition, that now benefits all Americans. From the time the law took effect through fall 1997, background checks had stopped 173,000 criminals and other high-risk purchasers from buying handguns, and the law has helped to reduce illegal gun trafficking.

Sarah was not pursuing fame, or even recognition. She simply started at one point—when our son, Scott, found a loaded handgun on the seat of a pickup truck and, thinking it was a toy, pointed it at Sarah.

Fortunately, no one was hurt. But seeing a gun nearly bring a second tragedy upon our family, Sarah became determined to do whatever she could to prevent senseless death and injury from guns.

Some people think of Sarah as a powerful political force. To me, she's the person who so many times fed me and helped me dress during my long years of recovery.

Overcoming obstacles is part of life, not just for people who are challenged by disabilities, illnesses, or tragedies, but for all people. No matter what the obstacle—fear, disability, prejudice, grief, or a difficulty that isn't likely to "just go away"—we can all work to make this world a better place.

Seen here in his track and field days at UCLA, Jackie Robinson was a multisport athlete. His talent and character always shone through despite a racist society that tried to smother them.

1

WHEN THE FIGHT WAS JUST BEGINNING

IN 1972, ROGER KAHN'S book *The Boys of Summer* was published. It detailed the amazing Brooklyn Dodgers team that won six pennants in the late 1940s and early 1950s, and won the 1955 World Series. At a book-signing party in New York City, former Dodgers teammates Carl Erskine and Jackie Robinson stood talking. Jackie remarked that he had recently quit playing golf because he couldn't see the ball anymore. Erskine took this as a joking comment aging athletes often make.

Then a woman approached with a copy of the book and a pen for Jackie. "Would you start my hand on the page so I don't go off the edge?" he quietly asked Erskine. That's when Erskine knew that Jackie wasn't kidding—he could hardly see at all. He suffered from diabetes and heart disease, making him appear tired and old, and causing him to walk with a limp. The illness had taken nearly all his eyesight.

But Jackie Robinson's beliefs were as strong as ever. In June 1972 he was invited to a pregame ceremony honoring him as the first African American in modern major league baseball. He was proud, he said, that so many black ballplayers were in the major leagues now.

But he also stated firmly, "I will not be satisfied until I look over at that dugout and see a black manager leading a team." He never lived to see that day.

Jackie Robinson was more than a good baseball player. He helped usher in a new era for African Americans of all walks of life. It was not easy, and Jackie faced more adversity, perhaps, than any other professional athlete of the 20th century. But he never gave up. His teammate Joe Black later commented: "The biggest thing I learned from Jackie—the fight is never over."

*   *   *

On January 31, 1919, Mallie Robinson gave birth to a son, Jack Roosevelt Robinson, in Cairo, Georgia. She and her husband, Jerry, already had four children—Edgar, who was 10; Frank, 9; Mack, 5; and Willa Mae, 4. The Robinsons lived on the same plantation where their ancestors had been slaves before the Civil War. As sharecroppers, they owed most of their crops to the white owner of the land and kept only a small portion as profit. Sharecroppers suffered a life of constant hard work and unrelenting debt. Before Jackie was born, Mallie had convinced Jerry to negotiate a better deal with the landlord: they would keep half the crops instead of a smaller portion.

But life was still hard for the couple, and when young Jackie was six months old, Jerry decided to seek his fortune elsewhere. He said he would go to Texas and try to find work, promising to send for Mallie and the children when he did. Jerry never came back and never sent for his family. Mallie struggled to keep up the farm work and still care for her five children. Finally, in 1920, when baby Jackie was 16 months old, the 30-year-old woman sold what few possessions she could and took her family to her brother Burton's home in Pasadena, California. Mallie hoped she could find better work for herself and build a better life for her children away from the extreme racism of the Deep South.

For two years Mallie and her children stayed in a three-

room apartment with Burton and his wife and family. Mallie was able to find housekeeping work, and after two years of hard work and scrimping, she saved enough to move her children to a house on Pepper Street. The family nicknamed the small, modest home "the Castle."

Racism, however, was everywhere, not just in the Deep South. Neighbors gathered signatures on petitions to keep the Robinsons out of the mostly white neighborhood. They even burned a cross on the Robinsons' lawn. But Mallie refused to give in to hatred and she stayed in her house. Her children learned not to give in, either. When Jackie was eight years old, a neighbor girl taunted him with racial

From his earliest days Jackie (second from left) felt his mother deserved a better life. She managed to raise five children on her own after her husband walked out on them.

slurs shouted across the yard. Jackie knew the worst name for white people in the South, "cracker," and he shouted it back. The girl ran into the house and soon her father emerged, cursing at Jackie for calling a white child names. The disturbance finally ended when the man's wife came outside and scolded him for fighting with an eight-year-old boy.

Jackie also learned that African Americans were not allowed to use the neighborhood YMCA facilities or the municipal pool, except occasionally. When he went to movies with his friends, he was required to sit in the balcony seats. In the movie theater, though, he found encouragement in films about boxing champion Joe Louis, "the Brown Bomber." Jackie and his friends idolized him. Louis was an athlete who competed with whites as an equal and won.

In the face of inequality, though, what hurt Jackie most was watching his mother work long hours at low-paying jobs to support her children. When his sister Willa Mae started school, there was no one to stay home with Jackie. The school would not allow him to attend because he was too young. So for a year, Jackie went to school with Willa Mae and sat outside in the sandbox until school let out at noon.

Mallie often worked 12-hour days, but she always found energy to spend time with her children. "I remember, even as a small boy, having a lot of pride in my mother," Jackie later wrote in his autobiography, *I Never Had It Made*. "I thought she must have had some kind of magic to be able to do all the things she did, to work so hard and never complain and to make us all feel happy. We had our family squabbles and spats, but we were a well-knit unit."

Even with Mallie's hard work, however, sometimes there was no food. The family got by on two meals a day, and the children would eat bread and drink sugar water when there was nothing else to be had. As a child Jackie, like his older siblings, helped out when he could. He cut grass, delivered newspapers, or performed other odd jobs, and then handed the money over to Mallie.

For recreation in the days before television and radio, neighborhood ball games abounded. Jackie would tag along with his brother Mack, a great player and a very fast runner. But the seven-year-old Jackie was never allowed to play, so he just watched Mack. One day the teams were short a player, and Mack suggested they let Jackie play. The kids were doubtful—he was so young and he'd never played baseball before. But they could either let Jackie play, or not play at all. Even so, they didn't let him take his turns at bat until his team was behind by two runs.

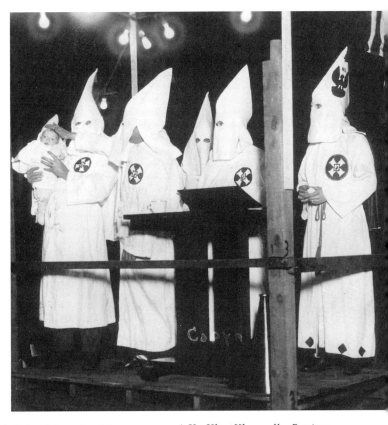

A Ku Klux Klan rally. Racism pervaded the America of Jackie Robinson's childhood. When his family moved to a mostly white section of Pasadena, neighbors burned a cross on their lawn.

Finally given an opportunity, Jackie smacked a double. When the next batter stepped up to the plate, Jackie stole third. When Jackie slid into home plate in a cloud of dust, the other kids decided he could play with them anytime. In grade school Jackie was already such a good athlete that kids at school would bribe him with lunch or money if he'd play on their team. Jackie gave the money to his mother.

Jackie found another kind of recreation in the Pepper Street Gang. Composed of other "outcast" children from ethnic groups that faced discrimination, the gang never committed serious crimes, but they did get into trouble. "[H]ardly a week went by when we didn't have to report

No one could deny Jackie's incredible talent. At UCLA he excelled at football, basketball, baseball, and track but left after just two years.

to Captain Morgan, the policeman who was head of the Youth Division," Jackie remembered.

They stole fruit from grocery stands or orchards, threw clumps of dirt at passing cars, and in general made other kinds of minor trouble. The gang members might steal golf balls from a nearby course or baseballs from a nearby field and sell the balls back when they had enough of them. Jackie once led his buddies in retaliating against a prejudiced neighbor: they put black tar on the man's lawn. When Mallie found out, she made Jackie go back and clean up the mess.

Another time the kids went swimming in the city reservoir. This incident saw Jackie and his friends taken to the sheriff at gunpoint. They were not arrested, but it was nevertheless humiliating. The deputies jeered at the kids and interrogated them for hours under hot lights. When the boys begged for a drink or something to eat, they brought in a watermelon, which the boys were forced to eat off the floor.

Jackie later credited a kindly neighborhood mechanic named Carl Anderson and a local minister named Karl Downs with turning him around. Anderson chatted with Jackie one day and pointed out that if he kept up his gang activities, Jackie would soon find himself arrested. That, Anderson said, would break Mallie's heart. He encouraged

Jackie to stop following the crowd and to be his own person. And Downs, a young, athletic minister, encouraged the neighborhood kids to participate in youth programs at the church. Badminton, dances, and other youth-oriented events helped the church attract younger members and families. Jackie counted Downs as a good friend and adviser; later on, Jackie taught Sunday school at the minister's church.

In the meantime, Jackie's sister Willa Mae was an accomplished athlete in the few sports that were open to girls: basketball, track, and soccer. And Jackie's brother Mack had become a sports star at John Muir Technical High School and then at Pasadena Junior College. In 1936, when Jackie was 17, his brother Mack competed in the Olympics in Munich. Mack won a silver medal in the 200-meter dash—he was beaten at the last second by the great Jesse Owens (who won four gold medals at the games). Jackie saw Mack as a great inspiration. "Even though doctors warned him that his participation in sports could be fatal because he had a heart ailment," Jackie said, "he wouldn't give up."

His other brother Frank made it to nearly all the games and events in which Jackie took part. "[M]y brother Frank was my greatest fan. He constantly encouraged and advised me. I wanted to win, not only for myself but also because I didn't want to see Frank disappointed," Jackie wrote. By the time he graduated from high school in 1937, he had earned letters in four sports: football, basketball, baseball, and track and field. Jackie and his family were disappointed that despite his tremendous athletic ability, his talent had not been rewarded with a college scholarship.

Mallie was adamant her children would attend college, despite her severely limited income. Jackie enrolled at Pasadena Junior College, determined to work hard—perhaps a scholarship would come after all. Jackie's first year at PJC was marred by a broken ankle suffered early in the football season. When it healed he played quarterback and led his team to five wins and one tie in the last six games. He immediately moved on to the basketball team, becoming the team's high scorer. When basketball ended, Jackie moved on to baseball and track.

Frank Robinson was particularly proud of a banner day in Jackie's school athletic career. A track meet and a championship baseball game were scheduled for the same day, 40 miles apart. Jackie arranged to be the first competitor at the track meet in Claremont. A flat tire resulted in Jackie's arriving early enough to compete but too late to warm up. Nevertheless, he won the long jump, breaking his brother Mack's record with a leap of 25 feet, $6\frac{1}{2}$ inches. Then he jumped back into his friend's car for the trip to the baseball game in Glendale. His team won the championship that day. Jackie was voted Most Valuable Junior College Player in Southern California in 1938.

As he was preparing to graduate from PJC, Jackie was offered a number of scholarships to big schools. He considered them carefully; the best of the lot was for a college very far away. Jackie decided on the University of California at Los Angeles (UCLA), in part so that he could remain near his family and help Mallie out whenever possible. His main reason for choosing UCLA, though, was so Frank could attend his sports events and cheer him on.

Unfortunately, tragedy struck the Robinson family. One night in May 1939 Frank was involved in a motorcycle accident, and he died the next morning. Jackie was heartbroken. "I was very shaken up by his death. It was hard to believe he was gone, hard to believe I would no longer have his support," Jackie later wrote. He consoled himself with the thought that Frank would want him to do well at college.

Jackie certainly did well at UCLA. He immediately became a star football player, but then, with only three games left in the season, he injured his ankle. Jackie played the final three games despite the pain. He took no time off after the season, either: basketball was next. Here, too, he excelled. He led the league in scoring. Then came baseball, in which he played shortstop, and track, in which he earned several medals and ribbons in broad jumps. By the end of his first year at UCLA, Jackie had earned four letters—the first UCLA student ever to do so. As if these achievements weren't enough, he had managed to hold down a part-time job, too.

He started his second year at UCLA in the same promising way, playing football and basketball and attracting a great deal of attention. He had also found a girlfriend, a freshman named Rachel Isum. Watching Jackie on the football field, strutting around with his hands on his hips, Rachel at first thought he was conceited and "stuck on himself." She soon changed her mind.

Jackie had a much different impression of her. "[W]hen I was with Rae I was delighted to find that I could tell her anything. She was always understanding and, beyond that, very direct and honest with me. . . . From the beginning I realized there was something very special about Rae."

Despite his feelings for Rachel Isum and despite the athletic honors he had won, Jackie felt he wasn't achieving very much at school. What's more, he worried about his ability to make a respectable living. "I felt I was living in an academic and athletic dream world," he later recalled. "I could see no future in staying at college, no real future in athletics." He also felt bad about his mother working so hard on her own and believed it "necessary for me to relieve some of my mother's financial burdens." UCLA even offered extra financial support if Jackie would stay on a bit longer. Although both Mallie and Rae wanted Jackie to stay and graduate, he decided to leave school after the basketball season ended.

Drafted into the army, Jackie faced as much racism in the military as he had in civilian life. He would find ways to change things as a lieutenant, especially when his men turned to him for leadership.

2

AN OFFICER AND A SHORTSTOP

JACKIE'S ATHLETIC ABILITIES were truly amazing. There was no doubt that he could compete and win at any level. But he knew that because of his race, few, if any, opportunities existed for him in professional sports. "I wanted to do the next best thing—become an athletic director," Jackie recalled. "The thought of working with youngsters in the field of sports excited me." So after leaving UCLA in the spring of 1941, Jackie found a job working with the National Youth Administration as an assistant athletic director at a camp in Atascadero, California. He found the work very rewarding. Most of the kids he coached were from poor families or broken homes, and because of his own experiences growing up, he felt specially able to encourage them to succeed.

Unfortunately for Jackie, World War II was raging in Europe, and although the United States was not involved, the National Youth Administration found many of its activities shut down. He tried to get a job playing one of the many sports in which he excelled, but he had no luck. "[N]o major football or basketball clubs hired black players," he later wrote. "The only job offered me was with the [minor league] Honolulu Bears," an integrated football team in Hawaii. When Jackie went there, he found a job during the week working with a construction company. On the weekends he earned $100 a game.

Still, by early December, Jackie was homesick and dissatisfied. He got on a ship bound for California on December 5. Two days later, the Japanese navy bombed the American naval base at Pearl Harbor, and the United States declared war. Sailors ran around Jackie's ship painting windows black to disguise the lights from passing aircraft.

Very soon Jackie was drafted into the army and sent to Fort Riley, Kansas, for basic training. Here he and some other black draftees applied for officer training. They were told they had been accepted, but they were not allowed to enroll. Jackie watched as the white soldiers enrolled and finished the course, while the African Americans who were accepted were held back. After three months of waiting, Jackie learned that one of his heroes, Joe Louis, had been transferred to Fort Riley. Jackie took the problem to Louis, the most famous African-American athlete of his time, who promised to do something about the injustice. Louis used his well-known name and wrote to officials in Washington about the situation. The army didn't want the bad publicity that was sure to ensue, and soon Jackie and fellow black soldiers were enrolled in Officer Candidate School. Jackie became a second lieutenant in January 1943 and was appointed morale officer of his battalion.

Soon his men came to him with a complaint. The post exchange at Fort Riley had only a few seats for black soldiers. The rest were reserved for whites. As a result, many black soldiers would be kept waiting for seats even if most of the seats were empty. The soldiers were upset by the discrimination, but they did not really believe Jackie could do much about it. He called an officer about the seating arrangement and was told there was nothing that could be done. He insisted though, and finally the officer at the

other end of the line said, "Lieutenant, let me put it to you this way. How would you like to have your wife sitting next to a nigger?"

Jackie exploded. "Every typewriter in headquarters stopped. The clerks were frozen in disbelief at the way I ripped into the major," he later recalled. His commanding officer heard the exchange and supported him. Eventually the problem of seating was resolved—at least partly. "More seats were allocated for blacks, but there were still separate sections for blacks and for whites," Jackie explained. "At least, I had made my men realize that something could be accomplished by speaking out, and I hoped

Jackie turned to heavyweight champ Joe Louis, who was also drafted, for assistance against racial injustice in the army. The two would meet again after their days in the service and try out the weapon of choice for each other's sport.

that they would be less resigned to unjust conditions." Throughout his life, his courage and persistence in protesting unfair conditions would set an example for other African Americans.

But at Fort Riley, his protest made him known to "higher-ups" as a troublemaker. It didn't help matters when Jackie was asked to play on Fort Riley's baseball team. Normally, the offer would have delighted Jackie. But many opposing teams refused to play on the same field as a black man, and the army wouldn't take a stand on the matter. If a team objected to Jackie's participation, the army expected him to sit out the game. Jackie had no intention of accepting these regulations. He refused to play at all. "They dropped the matter but I had no illusions," he wrote. "I would never win a popularity contest with the ranking hierarchy of that post." Sure enough, Jackie was soon transferred to Fort Hood, Texas—a post with a reputation for vicious racism.

At Fort Hood, Jackie was placed in charge of the 761st Tank Battalion, despite his knowing nothing about tanks. Nevertheless, he felt honesty with his men was the best way to approach the task. He explained to his men, who knew much more about tanks than he did, that he would have to rely on them for guidance and help. "The first sergeant and the men knocked themselves out to get the job done . . . our unit received the highest rating" of any on the post, Jackie wrote.

Shortly after this triumph, however, discrimination reared its ugly head once more. Jackie boarded an army bus and, seeing a friend, sat next to her. The bus driver, observing the very dark Jackie sitting with a light-skinned woman who he assumed was white, stopped the bus. He told Jackie to move to the back of the bus. But Jackie knew the army had recently outlawed segregated seating on any vehicles on army bases. The ruling had come as a result of the refusal of champion boxer Joe Louis to move to the back of a bus.

At the end of the bus route, Jackie was arrested by military police. He found the situation almost laughable. He said later, "I was naive about the elaborate lengths to which racists in the Armed Forces would go to put a vocal black man in his place." Lieutenant Robinson was court-martialed (put on trial by the army). Although Jackie was eventually cleared of all charges, he was "fed up with the service" and applied for an honorable discharge. In November 1944 he got it.

An acquaintance in the army suggested that Jackie try to get a job with the Kansas City Monarchs, a baseball team in the Negro leagues. Jackie wrote to the team and was accepted on a trial basis for spring training.

In the meantime, Jackie spent time with Rae in San Francisco. Rae had been in training to be a nurse while Jackie was in the army and in 1943 agreed to marry him when she finished school. However, when she wrote to Jackie saying she was thinking about serving as a nurse in the army, Jackie was adamant that she not do so. Rae, not one to be bullied, sent back the ring and bracelet Jackie had given her. The two made up while Jackie was home on leave, and after he left the army, Jackie was determined to make a decent living so he could marry Rae. Before the Monarchs' season began, he coached basketball at Sam Houston College in Texas—a job he found thanks to his old friend and mentor, the Reverend Karl Downs. Come spring, his job with the Monarchs would pay him $400 a month.

The money wasn't great, but for a black man seeking to make a living playing professional ball, a Negro leagues club such as the Monarchs was the only option. It hadn't always been that way. In the earliest days of baseball in the mid-1800s, minorities played alongside whites on professional teams.

All that changed in the late 1800s, when a general shift toward institutionalized prejudice began taking place in America; the late 1880s into the 1890s was the period

Rae agreed to marry Jackie soon after he was discharged from the army. A strong-willed individual, she became a source of strength to her husband throughout his career.

when most Jim Crow laws—requiring segregation—were passed. In 1887 the integrated International League decided to bar players of color; other mostly white leagues also stopped hiring African-American players.

In 1885 the first professional black baseball team was formed. Originally called the Argyle Hotel Athletics, the team met with local success and then decided to travel. Because of racial bias, particularly in the South, the team was renamed the Cuban Giants, and players pretended to speak Spanish on the field.

They beat several professional white teams, including the National League's Cincinnati and Indianapolis teams and even the champion Detroit team. Other professional black teams were formed, but many were not successful or lasted only a few seasons. By 1898 only one all-black professional team remained. "In 1899," author James Riley notes, "one black player, Bill Galloway, appeared in five games in the Canadian League. This marked the last time a black player appeared alongside whites in organized baseball" until nearly 50 years later.

There was never an official rule barring blacks from organized baseball after 1900. However, an unspoken understanding—a so-called gentlemen's agreement—existed from the turn of the century among major league team owners not to hire blacks.

In the absence of opportunities for black ballplayers in the major leagues, forward-thinking businessmen put together all-black professional teams during the first two decades of the 20th century. But while some of these teams played excellent baseball, none were part of an organized league. Each team scheduled its own games, and players could—and did—jump from one team to another as they wished.

If a major league team owner had been tempted to break the gentlemen's agreement—and there is no convincing evidence that any had—such thoughts would probably have been banished following the 1919 World Series. After the heavily favored Chicago White Sox were defeated by the Cincinnati Reds, it was discovered that a handful of White Sox players had taken money from gamblers to deliberately lose the Series. The incident, dubbed the "Black Sox" scandal, rocked baseball to its foundations. Many sportswriters questioned whether the game could even survive.

In response to the scandal, the major league club owners created the position of commissioner of baseball and hired an eminent federal judge, Kenesaw Mountain Landis, to fill it. Landis's mandate was to clean up the game, and he pursued his task vigorously. In 1921, after the eight players accused in the Black Sox scandal were acquitted in a criminal trial, the commissioner issued his own verdict, banning the players from organized baseball for life. The last thing the game needed at this time was another controversy. And there is no doubt that integrating the game would have created just that.

In any event, as Commissioner Landis was taking control of the white major leagues, another towering figure was ensuring that black ballplayers had a league of their own. In 1920 Rube Foster, a longtime star pitcher for various independent black baseball teams, spearheaded the creation of the National Association of Colored Professional Baseball Clubs (commonly known as the Negro National League). The eight-team league—of which Foster served as president, in addition to being a club owner—was modeled after the white major leagues. Foster believed that a successful Negro league would ultimately open the way for black stars in the major leagues.

In 1923 the Eastern Colored League became the second all-black baseball league. Other leagues followed. Financial and organizational problems often plagued these leagues, particularly during the early days of the Great Depression and after Foster's death in 1930. But black baseball ultimately survived and prospered, producing some of the best baseball players—black or white—in the history of the game. These stars included outfielder James "Cool Papa" Bell, perhaps the fastest ballplayer ever; slugger Josh Gibson, a catcher whose mammoth home runs earned him the nickname "the Black Babe Ruth"; and pitcher LeRoy "Satchel" Paige, who is believed to have hurled more than 50 no-hitters in his long career.

By the late 1930s, two black leagues, the Negro National League and the Negro American League, had risen to preeminence. In 1942 the two leagues played the first Negro World Series, during which the Negro American League champion Kansas City Monarchs defeated their National League counterparts, the Homestead Grays.

By 1945, when Jackie Robinson was invited to spring training by the Kansas City Monarchs, the team had lost many of its stars to the armed forces. Still, Jackie was joining one of the nation's best ball clubs. Of the first six Negro American League pennant races, the Monarchs had won five.

Best team or not, the Monarchs were black. To make enough money to stay in business, the Negro leagues teams had to play as many games as possible. Jackie found that schedules were unbelievably hectic. Sometimes the games were far apart but scheduled with little time in between. The teams could literally spend days on a bus, arrive to

The scandal of the 1919 Chicago "Black Sox" (above) rocked baseball to its foundation. It also may have delayed the integration of baseball, which many would have perceived as another scandal.

play a doubleheader, and the next day get back on the bus to travel another few hundred miles. Satchel Paige once remarked that he found it amusing to hear of major league pitchers complaining of overwork when they had to pitch more than three times a week. Paige himself pitched six or seven days a week—sometimes up to three games a day! There is no question Negro leagues ballplayers worked hard, and it showed in their excellent performances.

What perturbed Jackie more than the tight schedules were the conditions under which the players were forced to live, simply because they were black. Traveling was difficult at best when few hotels, restaurants, or even public rest rooms allowed African Americans. "You were lucky if they magnanimously permitted you to carry out some greasy hamburgers in a paper bag with a container of coffee," he recalled. "You were really living when you were able to get a plate of cold cuts. You ate on board the team bus or on the road." When the team did manage to stay in hotels that allowed blacks, they often found them dirty, in disrepair, and generally inadequate.

Just as he had in the army, Jackie challenged the conditions when he could, and encouraged his teammates to stand up for their rights and assert their dignity. At a service station in Oklahoma where the team had been stopping for gas for 30 years, Jackie got off the bus to use the bathroom. The owner would not allow him.

"Take the hose out of the tank," Jackie said. "If we can't use the bathroom here, we'll buy our gas someplace else." The owner thought a moment, then decided he probably couldn't sell a hundred gallons of gas anytime soon. The players were allowed to use the rest room.

"After that," Jackie's teammate Buck O'Neil remembered, "we always got off the bus to use the restroom wherever we stopped, and if we couldn't use the restroom we didn't buy the gas."

Jackie Robinson was happy to be earning a living playing baseball, but he deplored the segregation and racism that forced talented black ballplayers to work under such conditions and without the recognition or rewards of being in the major leagues. Still, he felt there was little choice. "If I left baseball," Jackie wrote, "where could I go, what could I do to earn enough money to help my mother and to marry Rachel?" Very soon Jackie would find the answer to that question.

In 1946 Jackie got one step closer to the major leagues when he signed with the Dodgers' top minor league team, the Montreal Royals. Many saw his signing as nothing more than a token. As he had done most of his life, he would prove the skeptics wrong.

3

A MONARCH
AND A ROYAL

JACKIE'S YEAR WITH the Kansas City Monarchs was nothing short of remarkable. He had the chance to learn from some of the greatest players in the game, such as the legendary Satchel Paige. Jackie took full advantage of the opportunity. By the end of the season, he led the team in batting at .345; he had 10 doubles, four triples, and five home runs. The team played 41 games with Jackie at shortstop. He was also the shortstop for the Negro leagues' West team in the all-star East-West game.

Brooklyn Dodgers scouts haunted Negro leagues games that season. When Clyde Sukeforth, the top scout for the Dodgers, approached Jackie in August, it was assumed that Sukeforth was scouting for a new team. The president of the Dodgers ball club, Branch Rickey, had announced he was starting a new team. The "Brown Dodgers" were to play in the new United States League while the Dodgers were away from Brooklyn. The new league, he said, would be organized differently from the existing Negro leagues; its teams would be more like major league clubs. Rickey was criticized by those who worked for integration in sports; they thought he was trying to take business away from the Negro leagues while still preserving segregation in major league baseball.

But Rickey was determined to break baseball's color line and sign some African-American talent to his team, though he knew he would face fierce opposition. The new team actually did play, but for just one season. Rickey later claimed the Brown Dodgers were his way of keeping negative attention away from his real plans. The new team allowed him to scout for the right player to break the color line without arousing too much attention—attention that could spoil the experiment.

As far as Jackie Robinson and his teammates knew, Sukeforth represented just another major league team pretending to be interested in hiring black players. The black players tried not to get their hopes up—they had been scouted by major league teams before. Earlier in 1945 black sportswriter Wendell Smith had arranged for Jackie and two other players to try out for the Boston Red Sox. The players had done well, but nothing had come of the tryout.

Rickey's scouts, including Sukeforth, had been looking at promising black ballplayers since 1943. They did not limit their search to the United States, either. Many black players, disgusted with conditions in the United States, played in countries like Mexico, Cuba, Puerto Rico, or Venezuela, where they faced less prejudice and made more money. Among the American stars in Rickey's file were Satchel Paige, Josh Gibson, and Cool Papa Bell, all of them outstanding, even legendary, players. But Rickey and his scouts were not looking just for athletic ability.

Rickey knew that the first black to make it to the major leagues had to have a solidly respectable character, above-average intelligence, and, even more important, courage. The player had to know that the hopes of all other black players would be pinned on him. His behavior on and off the field had to be impeccable. Rickey needed somebody who would not get involved in fistfights and start brawls. Such a man was difficult to find. Rickey knew that white players and fans would purposely try to stir him into arguments and even fights to make him look bad.

The 26-year-old Jackie Robinson had an undeniable talent on the field, but he was also an impressive individual off the field. Jackie was college educated, did not drink alcohol or use drugs, and had never dated "loose" women. He had worked and played sports with whites in Pasadena, at UCLA, and in the army. Rickey knew about the only "blot" on Jackie's record: his "racial agitation"—in other words, his defense of his own civil rights. Unlike many others who felt vocal blacks were a threat, Rickey believed Jackie's behavior had been just what any self-respecting man would have done, and it showed courage. If Jackie had been white, Rickey believed, "people would have said, 'Here's a guy who's a contender, a competitor.'"

Jackie's name was on the top of Rickey's list. But when Sukeforth caught up with the Monarchs in 1945, he couldn't watch Jackie play because Jackie had injured his shoulder. Nevertheless, Sukeforth invited Jackie to New York for a meeting with Branch Rickey.

In August 1945 Jackie went to New York. The discussion between Jackie and Rickey has become a legend. Rickey supposedly talked for hours, describing in graphic detail the kind of abuse Jackie would face, even acting out the parts. Players and fans would shout racial slurs; Jackie could not answer them. Pitchers would throw at his head, umpires would make unfair calls and throw insults in his face; Jackie could not react. Base runners would spike him with their shoes; Jackie could not retaliate. "They'll try to provoke a race riot in the ball park. This is the way to prove to the public that a Negro should not be allowed in the major league[s]. This is the way to frighten the fans and make them afraid to attend the games," Rickey said.

Hotel clerks, bus drivers, and all other kinds of people would try to push Jackie until he reacted so they'd have

Branch Rickey knew it would take much more than talent to break the color barrier in the major leagues. He tested Jackie's character in a legendary face-to-face meeting between the two.

reason to enforce segregation. He would get hate mail, even threats. On and off the field, he would face physical intimidation and abuse, and he could not fight back. Rickey asked that Jackie hold to this agreement not to retaliate for three years. At the same time, he could let none of this abuse shake his self-esteem or his confidence because his ball-playing abilities also had to be top-notch.

Rickey's graphic depictions of insulting characters almost made Jackie get up and take a swing at him. Finally Jackie asked, "Mr. Rickey, are you looking for a Negro who is afraid to fight back?" Rickey thundered, "I'm looking for a ballplayer with enough guts not to fight back!"

Rickey went on to say, "You've got to do this job with base hits and stolen bases and fielding ground balls, Jackie. *Nothing else*." Jackie was quiet for a few moments as he thought about the challenge. He questioned his own ability to turn the other cheek in the face of abuse, because he had always stood up for his rights and never backed down. But if it was for the greater good of all African Americans, Jackie decided he could do it.

Rickey later said that had Jackie answered immediately, without stopping to think, Rickey would have known that he was not the man to do the job. As it was, Rickey asked Jackie if he had a girlfriend. A little surprised at this personal question, Jackie answered that he thought so, but he hadn't seen her for some time. Rickey told Jackie not to tell anyone about the plan just yet, except for his mother and Rae. His job would be easier, Rickey told the player, if he had Rae by his side. Of course, Jackie had been planning to marry Rae anyway. But the news of his new job meant that he would now have the means to support Rae, and still take care of his mother. They planned to marry after Jackie returned from playing winter baseball in South America.

In October 1945, a few months after the meeting with Rickey, Jackie signed a contract to join the Montreal Royals in the spring of 1946. He would be paid $600 a month, with a $3,500 bonus for signing. The Montreal Royals were the top farm team of the Dodgers. (A farm team is a minor league club where new recruits sharpen their skills for the major leagues.) Many people, black and white alike, wondered if Jackie would really be brought up to the Dodgers, or if his place with the Royals was just window dressing. Either way, Jackie garnered a lot of attention when he joined the Royals. The attention was not always good.

Many popular white players, sportswriters, and club managers insisted that integration would never work. They gave various reasons for their opinions and predicted a players' strike or even racial violence. Most believed that Jim Crow laws, particularly in the South, would prevent Jackie from taking the field. Some said he would be so uncomfortable playing in the white leagues he would quit. Others asserted he just wasn't major league material; even his own teammates on the Kansas City Monarchs were divided about his abilities.

Of course, Jackie would have to pay his dues in the minor leagues first. Many players echoed the thoughts of Dixie Walker, who said, "As long as he isn't with the Dodgers, I'm not worried."

Some critics accused Rickey of merely using Jackie to make more money; a black player would lure black fans to Brooklyn and away from the Negro leagues. Rumors flew that the Kansas City Monarchs would sue Rickey for taking their player. These rumors were encouraged by some white team owners who wanted to prevent any blacks from playing in the major leagues. In addition, the Negro leagues rented major league stadiums, and any loss affecting their teams also affected the wallets of white major league owners.

One of the Monarch owners sent a telegram to Rickey denying that he wanted to prevent Jackie from playing in the major leagues. Still, the Dodgers organization never paid the Monarchs for signing away their player. The reality was that Jackie only had a verbal contract with the Monarchs; he agreed to play for them as long as he was paid every payday. (In later years, the Dodgers never paid for other talented black players either, including Dan Bankhead, Roy Campanella, Don Newcombe, Sandy Amoros, Joe Black, and Junior Gilliam.) Jackie himself remembered, "I guess the word got around that black fans would not view it kindly if the Jim Crow [Negro leagues] clubs barred the way for a black player to make the big time."

African-American fans, as well as players, were very excited. Here was the opportunity they all had hoped for:

if Jackie succeeded, the major leagues would be open to all minority players. What's more, many people of all races who weren't normally interested in baseball were excited. For decades, African Americans had struggled to achieve the rights to which all Americans were entitled. Blacks had fought with distinction in both world wars, and yet they were still second-class citizens in much of America. One famous cartoon showed two black soldiers with the caption, "Good Enough to Die for Their Country, But Not Good Enough for Organized Baseball." The segregation of baseball was just one area of inequality, but it was a highly visible one. A victory for African Americans in major league baseball would inevitably lead to victories elsewhere.

Before Jackie even got to spring training in 1946, the baseball world was buzzing. The thoughts of thousands of well-wishers were with him, but so too were the hopes of those who wanted to see him fail. Jackie didn't know it until later, but the manager of the Montreal Royals, Clay Hopper, begged Branch Rickey not to send a black player to his team. Hopper, born and raised in Mississippi, feared he'd be run out of his home state if he accepted Jackie. Rickey ignored his request.

After the end of the 1945 season with the Monarchs, Jackie played on a Negro National League all-star team in Venezuela. When he returned in January 1946, he and Rae made arrangements for their wedding. They were married on February 10, 1946, by Jackie's good friend, the Reverend Karl Downs.

Shortly afterward the couple left for spring training in Sanford, Florida. On the way there, in New Orleans, the Robinsons were bumped from a connecting flight to allow a white couple to travel. They were forced to wait 12 hours for the next flight and were denied service in the cafeteria. The next day, on their arrival in Pensacola, they were bumped from another flight. With nowhere to stay, they decided to take a bus, hoping to relax on the way to training; instead they were made to sit in the back of the bus on inferior seats.

Jackie seethed not only for himself but for his new wife. He inwardly questioned his ability to turn the other cheek as he'd promised. He later said that it was Rae's strength that kept him from exploding with rage. "[S]he wanted me to keep a tight grip on myself. . . . She would have more pride in me if I could follow through on Mr. Rickey's advice to suffer the loss of a few battles so that we could win a war."

With Jackie at spring training in Sanford was another black player, John Wright, who joined the Dodgers organization in February. Wright had played in the Negro leagues for the Pittsburgh Crawfords, the Newark Eagles, and the Homestead Grays before serving in the navy during the war. The two black players endured segregated housing in Florida, as well as the pressure of national attention. Their teammates, if not outwardly hostile, tended to avoid them. Both were pulled from an exhibition game in Sanford because of a local ordinance enforcing segregation. Rickey moved the team to Daytona Beach, where the local atmosphere was a little less hostile toward blacks.

Wright was a fine pitcher, Jackie later said, but the pressure to perform spectacularly got to him and he performed at less than his normal abilities that season. Wright finished the season with another Canadian league at Three Rivers, Quebec. The next season he returned to play with the Homestead Grays.

Jackie himself was, of course, determined to overcome the barriers placed in his way. He was the first black player in the International League since 1889 and the first in any recognized minor league since 1898. The pressure was intense. He was supported constantly by his wife, Rae, along with Rickey, Sukeforth, and even teammate Lou Rochelli, whom Jackie had replaced at second base. Rochelli, who might have been forgiven for being resent-

ful, kept up a one-man coaching program to help Jackie learn the new position. Manager Clay Hopper, despite his beliefs, was polite toward Jackie and careful to give him a fair chance.

In his first regular-season game with the Royals, against the Jersey City Little Giants, Jackie Robinson hit a home run and listened to the Giants' fans cheer him, an opposing player. By the end of the game, he had four hits in five at-bats and two stolen bases. His aggressive baserunning

Jackie and Rae tied the knot just before the couple left for Florida, where he would attend spring training with the Dodgers' top farm team. He was very protective of his wife; she helped him stay focused.

Jackie wasn't the only African-American player in his first year of spring training in 1946. Pitcher John Wright (fourth from left) wilted under the pressure, however.

so unnerved the opposing pitchers that they balked (stopped in the middle of a pitch, which is illegal) twice, allowing Jackie to walk home. In the field at second base, he made no errors. The Royals won this game and two more in Jersey City, thanks in part to Jackie.

But Jackie's excellent athletic skills did not win everyone over. In Jacksonville, Florida, the ballpark was locked to prevent him from playing with white players. In De Land, Florida, the team wasn't allowed to play, supposedly because the stadium lights were not working—yet it was a daytime game. In Syracuse, New York, Jackie faced the most vicious racial taunting he had seen. When he came up to bat, the opposing team threw a black cat out of the dugout and shouted, "Hey, Jackie, here's your cousin!" Jackie hit a double and eventually scored. On his way by the dugout, he shouted back, "I guess my cousin's pretty happy now!"

"The toll that incidents like these took was greater than I realized," Jackie later recalled. "I was overestimating my stamina and underestimating the beating I was taking. I couldn't sleep and often I couldn't eat." But he refused to back down. When a doctor prescribed rest and said Jackie was headed for a nervous breakdown, Jackie sat out for only one day before going back to the game. He knew all eyes were on him, and he wanted to avoid anyone saying he had "chickened out."

Vicious abuse was also flung at Jackie in Louisville, Kentucky, during the Little World Series, the International League championship. The Royals lost two of the three games played in Louisville.

But when they returned to Montreal to play the rest of the series, the team was delighted to find that fans were solidly behind them—and against Louisville. When the Louisville team came out of the dugout, Jackie recalled, the fans let "loose an avalanche of boos. . . . All through that first game, they booed every time a Louisville player came out of the dugout. . . . When we came on the field, our loyal Canadians did everything but break the stands down. . . . The confidence and love of those fans acted like a tonic to our team."

Boosted by the show of support from their fans, the Montreal Royals won three games in a row to take the series. Amidst the jubilant celebration, manager Clay Hopper approached Jackie and shook his hand, saying, "You're a great ballplayer and a fine gentleman. It's been wonderful having you on the team."

At the end of the last game, Jackie said, "[I] was thrilled but I was also in a hurry." He had to catch a plane to Detroit, where he would start off a month of barnstorming games.

Crossing the plate after hitting a home run in his debut with Montreal, Jackie is congratulated by one of the teammates he knocked in. Jackie led the team to the minor league championship that year.

Jackie was chased down the street by thousands of jubilant fans who had waited for him outside the locker room. "It was probably the only day in history that a black man ran from a white mob with love instead of lynching on its mind," said sportswriter Sam Martin.

Despite racial taunts and discrimination both on and off the field, Jackie Robinson had surpassed expectations in his season with the Royals. He led the International League in batting average (.349) and fielding percentage (.985) and tied for the league lead with 113 runs scored. His 40 stolen bases was second in the league. For his stellar performance, Jackie was voted Most Valuable Player in the International League.

But baseball wasn't the most important thing in Jackie's life in 1946. On November 18, Rae gave birth to a baby boy, Jack Roosevelt Robinson Jr.

Branch Rickey and Jackie sit down to make it official—Jackie is going to the major leagues. Though he had experienced much racism in the International League, Jackie could not have been prepared for the abuse that awaited him from fans, opposing players, and even some of his own teammates.

4

JACKIE PUTS A FOOT IN THE DOOR

IN THE SPRING OF 1947, close followers of baseball had some inkling of what was happening in the sport when the Dodgers and the Montreal Royals began spring training together—in Cuba, instead of the traditional location in Florida. The two teams played each other in seven exhibition games. The big announcement came five days before the Dodgers' first game of the season. Jackie had been promoted to the majors. It had happened. An African-American man would play major league baseball that year, for the first time in the 20th century.

Branch Rickey had spent the off-season of 1946–47 working with black community leaders in Brooklyn. He wanted to avoid any racial incidents that might give fuel to anti-integrationist fires. "There must be no gloating by Negroes when Robinson [is] brought up to the Dodgers, no 'Jackie Robinson Days', no wining and dining of the young ballplayer until he [is] fat and futile on the field," Rickey told them. Rickey also hoped to avoid possible race riots or fights in the stands. "Don't Spoil Jackie's Chances" became the rallying cry of the black community in New York and other cities where the Dodgers played.

For Jackie, the off-season meant spending time with his wife and new baby son. It was a welcome break from the pressures of the previous baseball season.

But trouble began again in spring training, and some of it came from his own future teammates. Dixie Walker, Eddie Stanky, Hugh Casey, Bobby Bragan, and Carl Furillo were among the mostly Southern players who wrote up a petition saying that they would rather be traded than play baseball with a black man. To their credit, some teammates, such as Pee Wee Reese and Gil Hodges, refused to sign. When manager Leo Durocher got wind of the petition, he was furious. He woke up all the players in the middle of the night and assembled them in their pajamas for a lecture.

"I hear some of you fellows don't want to play with Robinson and that you have a petition drawn up that you're going to sign," Durocher began. "Well, boys, you know what you can do with that petition. You can wipe your ass with it." The most important thing to the Dodgers, he said, was winning pennants, and Jackie Robinson was a great baseball player. "He's going to win pennants for us. He's going to put money in your pockets and money in mine." Branch Rickey, for his part, offered to trade any Dodger who refused to play with Jackie. (He later made good on his promise when Dixie Walker was traded to Pittsburgh.)

That was the end of the petition, but it was still some time—a very uncomfortable time for Jackie—before his teammates really accepted him. At first, they acted either indifferent or, like Eddie Stanky, genuinely hostile. Stanky told Jackie to his face, "[B]efore I play with you I want you to know I don't like it. I want you to know I don't like you." Jackie replied calmly, "All right. That's the way I'd rather have it. Right out in the open." Other teammates wouldn't speak to him at all or even sit with him; some avoided him, genuinely but naively thinking he'd rather be alone. To make matters worse, Jackie regularly received letters threatening murder, kidnapping of Jackie Jr., or

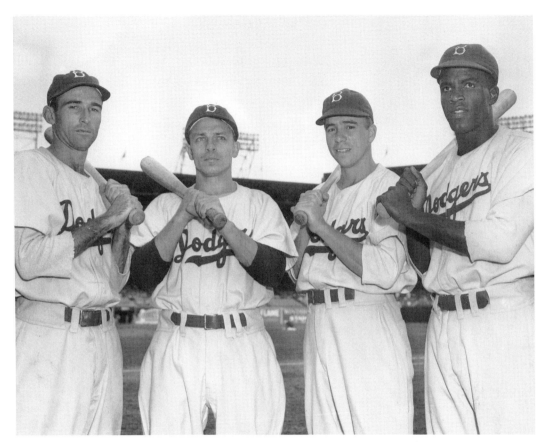

assaults on his wife.

Again Jackie found encouragement from Rae and from Branch Rickey, who told him to forget all the good work he had done for the Royals the year before. None of that mattered in the big leagues. "I want you to be a whirling demon against the Dodgers," Rickey said during spring training, before a Royals game with them. "I want you to concentrate, to hit that ball, to get on base *by any means necessary*. I want you to run wild, to steal the pants off them, to be the most conspicuous player on the field—but conspicuous only because of the kind of baseball you're playing." And Jackie did just that. In seven Royals-Dodgers games during spring training, Jackie batted an astounding .625 and stole seven bases.

The expressions in this photo of Jackie with (from left) Spider Jorgenson, Pee Wee Reese, and Eddie Stanky revealed plenty. Stanky was one of the most outspoken against playing with Jackie, though Reese eventually became a friend.

It took a lot for Jackie to pose for a snapshot with Phillies manager Ben Chapman after the Philadelphia squad had offered up some of the worst verbal abuse ever endured by Jackie. The incident may have ultimately helped Jackie bond with his teammates, however.

After the public announcement of Robinson's place on the Dodgers, the team opened its regular season at Ebbets Field in Brooklyn. Unfortunately, Jackie went hitless in his major league debut. In fact, he began the season mired in a slump. For the first five games, he didn't get a single hit in 20 at-bats. He began to lose confidence in himself. Leo Durocher had been suspended for the year (for keeping company with known gamblers), but his replacement, Burt Shotton, kept up Jackie's spirits with patience and encouragement. Then, in a three-game series against the Philadelphia Phillies, Jackie was subjected to the most severe taunting he had ever heard—in addition to the usual beanballs and spikings.

The Phillies' manager, Ben Chapman, reportedly told his team there would be a $5,000 fine for anyone who didn't go after Robinson. A stream of abuse flowed from the Phillies' dugout. Knowing about the death threats Jackie had received, the players held their bats up like guns and made machine-gun noises.

"Hey, nigger, why don't you go back to the cotton field where you belong?"

"They're waiting for you in the jungles, black boy!"

"Hey, snowflake, which one of those white boys' wives are you dating tonight?"

"We don't want you here, nigger!"

"[T]his day," Jackie later wrote, "of all the unpleasant days in my life, brought me nearer to cracking up than I ever had been." Still in his slump, Jackie couldn't manage to hit anything. Finally, in the eighth inning, Jackie hit a single. Then he stole second, stole third, and scored on the next batter's hit. The Dodgers won that game, but the abuse did not let up; if anything, it got worse.

Some amount of taunting was expected for rookies, no matter what color they were. In fact, Chapman would later claim he and his team were only shouting at Jackie the way they'd shout at any other player, just to throw off his concentration. But by the third game, Jackie's teammates had finally had enough. Eddie Stanky screamed at the Phillies dugout, "Listen, you yellow-bellied cowards, why don't you yell at somebody who can answer back? There isn't one of you has the guts of a louse!"

Newspapers had a field day with the Phillies' manager's offensive behavior. Chapman was warned by baseball commissioner Happy Chandler that race-baiting would not be tolerated. Chapman tried to save his job and his team's image by posing for a photograph with Robinson. Even so, Chapman refused to shake Jackie's hand, and instead the two posed holding a bat between them. "I have to admit

Though his popularity crossed color lines on the field, many whites treated Jackie with racist attitudes off it. Despite this strange attitude, he remained very obliging to all fans.

that having my picture taken with this man was one of the most difficult things I had to make myself do," Jackie said.

Rickey, ever the businessman, had a different take on the Chapman incident. Jackie later learned that the Phillies' president, Bob Carpenter, had tried to get Rickey to keep him out of the lineup for the games, by threatening that the Phillies would refuse to play. Rickey said that would be all right—the Dodgers would win all three games by forfeit. "Chapman did more than anybody to unite the Dodgers," Rickey declared. "[H]e solidified and unified thirty men, not one of whom was willing to sit by and see someone kick around a man who had his hands tied behind his back."

It wasn't just the Phillies who had it in for Jackie and the Dodgers. The Boston Braves jeered not only Jackie, but Pee Wee Reese too. Reese was a Southerner and had been raised in a culture of segregation and deep-seated prejudice. Reporters asked Reese before Jackie joined the team how he'd feel if a Negro took his job as shortstop. Reese was reasonable. "If he can take my job," he said, "he's welcome to it." Still, Reese and Jackie were not particularly friendly during the early part of the season. Now the Boston Braves and their fans shouted at Pee Wee, chiding him for being a Southerner and playing on a team with a black man. Reese didn't respond—except to walk over to Jackie and put a hand on his shoulder, saying a few friendly words. The jeers stopped immediately. More importantly, the gesture led to a long friendship between the two teammates.

In May the public heard about an attempt by some St. Louis Cardinals to start a players' strike in the National League. The strike would, of course, protest Jackie Robinson's place as a major leaguer. When the president of the league, Ford Frick, heard about this, he nipped the strike in the bud in no uncertain terms. He told the ringleaders:

> I do not care if half the league strikes. Those who do it will encounter quick retribution. They will be suspended, and I don't care if it wrecks the National League for five years. This is the United States of America, and one citizen has as much right to play as another. The National League will go down the line with Robinson whatever the consequence.

When the Dodgers finally did face the Cardinals, Jackie played first base. On one play Cardinals outfielder Enos Slaughter was tagged out but Slaughter kept running—toward Jackie, not the base. Jackie's thigh was badly cut when Slaughter spiked him. Fortunately the injury did no permanent damage and, like the Phillies incident, it unified the Dodgers. Some of Jackie's teammates had to be held back from pounding Slaughter. The Dodgers went on to beat the Cardinals in two of three games.

By the end of the 1947 season, Jackie Robinson had triumphed on the field, proving wrong the opponents of integrated sports. The Dodgers won the National League pennant, their first since 1941, with a record of 94 wins and 60 losses. Jackie himself, after busting out of his early slump, batted .297, led the team with 29 stolen bases and 125 runs, and tied with Pee Wee Reese for the team-high number of home runs, 12. Under normal circumstances, his stats would be considered excellent. Under the pressure Jackie faced that year, his performance was truly astounding.

Brooklyn lost the World Series to the Yankees that year—as it would in several years to come—but Jackie took home the Rookie of the Year Award. The award was given by the *Sporting News*—a publication that at the beginning of the year said Jackie wouldn't make it. But his performance had changed the minds of thousands of doubtful baseball fans as well as sportswriters. His exciting style of play electrified the baseball world.

Jackie was responsible for record-breaking game attendance in 1947—in Brooklyn, of course, but also in Pittsburgh, Philadelphia, Cincinnati, and Chicago. His mere presence on a major league team may have drawn many African-American baseball fans to the ballpark at first. But it was his daring, competitive style and his talent as a ballplayer that kept the fans coming—and would help make the Dodgers champions year after year.

Jackie's situation at the end of the season was not all rosy, though. The unrelenting pressure to succeed, the knowledge that all eyes were on him, and the herculean effort of not responding to vicious baiting left Jackie with an ulcer. He was also worried about the effect of his position on his wife and infant son. Despite Jackie's newfound status as a public hero, the Robinson family still had to fight discrimination in housing, restaurants, and other facets of life.

At the start of Jackie's first season with the Dodgers, Jackie, Rae, and their baby son had lived in a hotel room in New York. It was difficult to make new friends in the city and there was no one to rely on for babysitting. Rae often took young Jack Jr. to the games with her, warming his bottles at hot dog stands. By the end of the season, though, Rae found a more suitable apartment in Brooklyn, with two bedrooms and their own kitchen.

A visit from Jackie's friend Karl Downs helped lift the Robinsons' spirits. Unfortunately, Downs became ill during one Dodgers game and Rae had to take him to the hospital. After he recovered, he went back home to Texas. But he had not recovered after all. He underwent surgery in Texas in a segregated hospital. When there were complications following the surgery, instead of being carefully watched, he was promptly sent back to the Negro ward. Downs died from the complications. Jackie was heartbroken, and he was infuriated by the knowledge that if Downs had had surgery in Brooklyn at an integrated hospital, he probably would have survived. The surgeon was pressured to leave town, but that was little consolation for Downs's family and friends.

At the turn of the 21st century, it might be easy to think that Jackie Robinson's achievement was inevitable. In 1947 nothing could have been further from the truth. Jackie became the first black man in an all-white, nationally recognized, and prestigious league. Even more than today, baseball was then a patriotic institution in a country that prides itself on democracy and the equality of all people. Yet it was, like the society it represented, vehemently exclusionary.

Jackie, as a team member of the Dodgers in 1947, was at the forefront of the civil rights movement in America. He had to fight hard to earn his place in a highly visible profession. He did so alone a year before the American armed forces were integrated, 8 years before school segregation was outlawed, and 17 years before the Civil Rights Act was passed.

Jackie shows off his National League Most Valuable Player Award. His stellar performance was the key to major league owners' opening the door to other black ballplayers.

5

PUSHING THE
DOOR WIDE OPEN

PERHAPS THE BEST REWARD for Jackie's hard work in 1947 was that more black baseball players were signed to major league teams or farm clubs starting in July of that year. Larry Doby became the first African-American player in the American League when Bill Veeck signed him to the Cleveland Indians. In August, two black players from the Kansas City Monarchs, Willard Brown and Henry Thompson, were signed by the St. Louis Browns. Both soon returned to the Monarchs, but Thompson later played for the New York Giants from 1949 to 1956. About 16 more black players, according to author Robert Peterson, were signed to major league farm clubs in 1947, half of them by the Dodgers. Jackie's excellent performance and superhuman restraint opened the door to major league baseball for every minority player. By 1949 there were 36 black players in major league organizations (including farm clubs). Most of these were with the Cleveland Indians or the Brooklyn Dodgers organizations.

It was encouraging, but not enough. By 1950 only five major league teams were integrated, and it wouldn't be until 1959, 12 years after

Jackie's first season with the Dodgers, that the last major league team signed a black player. Ironically, that team was the Boston Red Sox, which could have been first to sign an African American when Jackie Robinson tried out for them in 1945. Not until 1974 was the first African American hired as a team manager (Frank Robinson of the Cleveland Indians). To this day there are no African-American owners of a major league baseball team.

Jackie Robinson's achievement in opening the doors to the major leagues also sounded the death knell for the mostly black-owned Negro leagues clubs. It began almost instantly. In 1947 attendance at Negro leagues games was down, and 1948 was much worse. At the end of that season, the Negro National League folded.

It wasn't that players suddenly performed badly; on the contrary, the real stars of Negro baseball were all still in the Negro leagues. Rather, the reason was that all eyes were on the Dodgers and specifically on Jackie Robinson beginning in 1947. The Dodgers' Ebbets Field stadium sold out game after game. "Jackie's nimble / Jackie's quick / Jackie's making the turnstiles click," exulted Wendell Smith of the *Pittsburgh Courier*. The other black players on major league farm clubs also garnered much attention from black baseball fans. Attendance at Negro leagues games plummeted despite their star players, and the teams couldn't afford to stay in business. Rube Foster's creation, originally formed to give black players the necessary experience and skills to compete in the white major leagues, had achieved its goal.

The Negro American League struggled on, but attendance kept shrinking and teams kept folding. The clubs' main source of income became selling the contracts of their players to the major leagues. When major league and farm teams began recruiting young players right out of school, the league could no longer attract talented black ballplayers. By 1960, only four teams were left in the Negro American League: Kansas City, Detroit–New

Orleans, Birmingham, and Raleigh, North Carolina. At the end of the season, they, too, folded.

Though the loss of the Negro leagues was unfortunate, progress was more important. "There are few to mourn at the grave of Negro baseball," author Robert Peterson asserts. "Old timers may wax nostalgic . . . but their voices mix pride with sorrow that these men labored behind the lily-white curtain" of the major leagues.

Of course, Jackie Robinson was not finished with baseball yet. Jackie spent the off-season on a speaking tour throughout the South. The hospitality he received from the black community during the tour was wonderfully encouraging to him. Unfortunately for him and the Dodgers, "We ate like pigs, and for me it was disastrous," Jackie remembered. When he reported for spring training, he was 25 pounds overweight. This may not sound like a big deal, but for a professional athlete just a few pounds is enough to reduce speed and flexibility, making the crucial difference between a winning play and a ruinous one.

Manager Leo Durocher, who had returned at the end of his one-year suspension, criticized Jackie and put him on a tough training schedule to take off the weight. Durocher was a good manager, and he did his job well, but he was not well liked or popular. He tended to be sarcastic and a bit of a loudmouth. Comments by Durocher about Jackie's weight got into newspapers and left the impression that Jackie had a "big head" now that he had finished his first major league season. Still, Jackie said later of Durocher, "There have been a lot of stories around that we don't like each other. The argument over my weight contributed to the belief that we had a feud going. This wasn't true." Jackie knew he was wrong to have allowed himself to gain weight and he worked hard to take it off fast.

The rest of the team worked hard, too, but in 1948 the

Larry Doby was the first African American to break the color barrier in the American League. Like Jackie Robinson, Doby would be elected to baseball's Hall of Fame.

Along with teammate Roy Campanella, Jackie took a job at the YMCA to stay in shape during the off-season. In the process, he exercised a genuine interest in working with the community and with children.

Dodgers were plagued with bad luck and injuries. Jackie was moved to second base, and in this position he worked hard with Reese, the shortstop, to develop his fielding skills. The Dodgers played a number of successful exhibition games in the Deep South and set attendance records, but Jackie developed a sore arm. After he recovered enough to play again, he accidentally collided with an opposing player, who was knocked unconscious. Jackie himself strained his left knee tendons. "[B]y the end of May," he remembered, "the Dodgers' hopes were really low."

Then Durocher was replaced by Burt Shotton as manager of the Dodgers. The change seemed to jump-start the team, which showed improvement over the previous year. Ultimately, though, the 1948 season was a disappointing one for the Dodgers. Jackie batted .296 for the season, just one point lower than his rookie average. He also hit 12 home runs and knocked in 85 runs. In the field, Jackie settled in to his new position, and he and Reese became an excellent double-play combination. But the Dodgers finished in a disappointing third place that year.

Still, there was much reason to be encouraged about the progress that baseball was making. One event in 1948—according to Jackie, the most important event—showed the changes occurring in people's attitudes toward black players. In Pittsburgh the Dodgers had "bench jockeyed," or heckled, an umpire for what they felt was a bad call. The umpire gave them a warning, but Jackie continued to heckle. The umpire turned, tore off his mask, and shouted, "Yer out of the game!" Jackie Robinson was thrown out for doing what ballplayers do. "That made me feel great, even though I couldn't play anymore that day," he recalled. "One of the newspapers said it in the best headline I ever got: JACKIE JUST ANOTHER GUY." The atmosphere was changing just as Branch Rickey had predicted.

After the 1948 season, Jackie took a job at the Harlem YMCA to make sure he was in top physical shape when spring training came around. He also found satisfaction and fulfillment in coaching again. At the YMCA that winter, Jackie helped disadvantaged young people work on physical fitness and develop their talent for sports. As he planned, he started the 1949 season in top condition, and it was far and away his best in baseball.

At the same time four more black players joined the Dodgers, which was encouraging to Jackie in particular. Dan Bankhead, Don Newcombe, Roy Partlow, and an excellent catcher named Roy "Campy" Campanella rounded out the 1949 Dodgers roster.

Jackie was also looking forward to the season for another reason: counting his year in Montreal, he had played his three seasons under Rickey's guidance, and now he was freed from his agreement. Jackie could now

His escalating fame never got in the way of Jackie's role as a family man. Here he helps Jackie Jr. after his son blew out the candles for his third birthday.

argue with umpires. He could answer back when insulted, just as any player would do. He could give free rein to his competitive spirit. The knowledge that the day was coming for his "emancipation," as he called it, helped him get through the tough times in those first three seasons. Now the day had arrived, and Jackie took full advantage of his freedom to be himself again.

In spring training Jackie refused to take some abuse from a rookie. This time he gave it right back to the player. He also proudly told reporters what he expected from other players that season: "They'd better be rough on me this year, because I'm sure going to be rough on them."

Commissioner Happy Chandler heard about the incident and reprimanded Jackie. He was worried such behavior could cause race riots during the season. But Jackie stood his ground. "I told the commissioner exactly how I felt and that while I had no intention of creating problems," he said, "I was no longer going to turn my cheek to insults."

Ironically, freed from playing the role of a docile black man, Jackie was criticized for supposedly being a hothead. The problem was that his refusal to retaliate in the early years despite appalling treatment had made him something of a saint, particularly to whites. People were shocked to hear him answer back some insults from his old nemesis Ben Chapman in 1949: "You son of a b——, if you open your mouth one more time I'm going to kick the s—— out of you."

The reality was that Jackie was merely giving as good as he got. This kind of behavior is common on the field of competition. But in 1949 many people didn't see it that way. Jackie noted later, "[T]he minute I began to answer, to argue, to protest . . . I became a swellhead, a wise guy, an 'uppity' nigger. When a white player did it, he had spirit. When a black player did it, he was 'ungrateful,' an upstart, a sorehead."

The controversy did not affect Jackie's performance on the field—if anything, his freedom gave him even more power as a competitive player. His daring and speed encouraged his teammates as well as attracted fans.

Jackie's famous daring style was not all his own. Negro leagues star Buck O'Neil remarked, "Jackie brought Negro baseball to the major leagues." He became so famous early on for base-stealing—a tactic not normally seen in the major leagues but ever-present in the Negro leagues—that more than one pitcher balked and made errors just because Jackie was on base. Sportswriter Roger Kahn remarked that Jackie's "bunts, his steals and his fake bunts and fake steals humiliated a legion of visiting players." Jackie got angry at opposing players' racial slurs, but he managed to use his anger to make him a better player. His teammate Duke Snider recalled Jackie's competitive spirit and daring baserunning in a particularly vivid anecdote:

Sam Jones [of the Chicago Cubs] was pitching, and we were down by one run, and he was throwing hard, and we weren't hitting him. Jackie came up [to bat], and he threw a close pitch, and Jackie started jawing at him, calling him gutless and screaming that he would beat him by himself. Jones got real hot and he hit Jackie with the next pitch. Jackie just got up laughing and jogged to first base. . . . "I'm gonna steal, I'm gonna steal," he's yelling at [Jones]. Sure enough, he steals second. "I'm gonna steal third, I'm gonna steal third." Then, in a flash, he has third stolen. By now you can fry an egg on old Sam's face, he's so mad. "I'll steal home, I'll steal home," and he makes one of those breaks, and Jones bounces the ball in the dirt. Jackie scores and we win the game by one run.

By the end of the 1949 season, Jackie Robinson was the acknowledged star player of the Brooklyn Dodgers. He led the league with a .342 batting average and 37 stolen bases. He was also among the league leaders in hits (203), runs scored (122), and runs batted in (124). Even more remarkable was that Jackie played with an injured foot ligament from August on. If he had been healthy all year, his statistics for the season might have been even higher. "He turned more double plays than any second baseman in the National League, often converting seemingly impossible plays into routine outs," author Richard Scott wrote. Jackie played second base for the National League All-Star team that year. He was a major force in bringing the Dodgers their second pennant in three years. The other team members were no slouches, either. His teammates Roy Campanella and Don Newcombe, for example, were also All-Stars. Despite their talent, the Dodgers lost the World Series yet again to the New York Yankees. Devoted Brooklyn fans merely shouted their refrain, "Wait till next year!" at their crosstown rivals.

Jackie received several plaques and citations that year, including the Most Valuable Player Award, voted upon by the sportswriters of the nation. (His fellow African-

American teammate Roy Campanella was voted the 1949 Rookie of the Year.) Jackie's phenomenal success earned him a 1950 contract with the Dodgers for a salary of $35,000, more than anyone else on the team had ever been paid.

Meanwhile, the Robinson family had other reasons to be proud and happy. They were finally making a home for themselves in their duplex in Flatbush, Brooklyn. When their landlady first rented to the Robinsons, she'd had to fight petitions from some of her white neighbors who were reluctant to see more blacks move in. But Jackie Jr. was a charming young boy who won over some of the skittish neighbors.

Other neighbors were starry-eyed over the great Jackie Robinson living there. One young white neighbor would sit outside the house and stare at Jackie, who was uncomfortable with the situation until he talked to the boy and realized he was a fan who just wanted some attention. "I couldn't have had a better little buddy," Jackie later wrote.

Another neighboring family, the Satlows, became good friends with Rae, Jackie, and Jackie Jr. As the Robinsons assembled their Christmas tree one winter, Jackie noticed the Satlow kids watching in awe. He thought the family couldn't afford their own tree, and in a gesture of friendship, he and Rae delivered another tree and half of their own decorations to the Satlow house. But the family only sat staring at it. Finally Sarah Satlow said, "We appreciate your thoughtfulness but, you see, you and Jack must have forgotten that we don't celebrate Christmas . . . being Jewish." The Robinsons were mortified, but soon everyone saw the humor in the situation, and the Satlows kept a Christmas tree that year. The two families became life-long friends.

But the best news that year for the Robinson family was that Jackie Jr. was going to have a sister. Sharon Robinson was born in January 1950.

Stealing home is a rarity in baseball and almost unheard of in the World Series. Jackie Robinson did it successfully in the 1955 fall classic, which the Dodgers went on to win.

6

STEALING HOME

BY 1950 JACKIE ROBINSON was not only a bona fide celebrity for his achievements on the baseball diamond, he was a role model in other ways. A devoted husband and caring father, Jackie was a religious man and a fighter. In the early 1950s his outspokenness both on and off the diamond made him a controversial figure, as well as a high-profile spokesperson for racial justice.

For example, for years when the team was in St. Louis white players on the Dodgers stayed at one hotel, while their black teammates stayed elsewhere. In 1953 Jackie demanded that the hotel allow him and his black teammates to stay. All team members should be treated equally, he reasoned, and if the hotel didn't like it, the Dodgers would stay elsewhere. The hotel, unwilling to be the target of bad publicity, gave in to Jackie's demand. Similarly, in a hotel in Cincinnati, he refused to continue eating his meals in his room and demanded service in the hotel restaurant. He knew if they served him, other African Americans would soon be welcome there.

His outspokenness had begun in his childhood, and was then

forcefully suppressed during his early years with the Dodgers. But in 1949 Jackie was among several black public figures invited to Washington, D.C., to testify before the House Un-American Activities Committee (HUAC). Anti-Communist fervor was sweeping the United States, and the African-American singer and actor Paul Robeson had made a statement that disturbed American politicians. Robeson had left the United States to live in England in 1931, disgusted at the way he had been treated in his own country because of his race, despite his celebrated talents. He visited the Soviet Union several times and found a very different situation there. Because of his own experiences, Robeson announced from Paris that American blacks should not serve in a war against the Soviet Union.

Jackie thought long and hard about the invitation before accepting. In his testimony before HUAC, Jackie said he believed Robeson had a right to his own opinion. But, he said, neither Robeson, himself, nor any other individual could speak for all African Americans. Having served in the army himself, Jackie declared that African Americans were certainly willing to serve their country. "But that doesn't mean that we're going to stop fighting race discrimination in this country until we've got it licked," he said. "We can win our fight without the Communists and we don't want their help." The statements endeared him to anti-Communists in the United States and increased his already great popularity.

After the birth of his daughter Sharon in January 1950, Jackie spent a few weeks in Hollywood before the season opened. *The Jackie Robinson Story* was being filmed, in which Jackie played himself, opposite Ruby Dee as Rae. He took Jackie Jr. with him so that Rae could recover from childbirth and an illness afterwards. But soon he missed her and his new daughter, so the girls of the family went west to be with Jackie. The family enjoyed the experience, particularly the star treatment they received. The film received bad reviews from some critics, and Jackie felt it would have been a better movie had it been made later in his career—and with a bigger budget. Nevertheless, he earned $50,000 plus royalties—a substantial sum at the time—for his work in the film.

During the 1950 season, stardom took its toll. Jackie learned that the bigots who opposed integrated sports were at work again. He received a death threat before a game at Cincinnati's Crosley Field, the first threat since the 1947 season. The police and the FBI were called in to ensure the safety of Jackie and his Dodgers teammates. Before the game his teammates joked that all of them should wear number 42 on their shirts to confuse any possible snipers. During the game teammate Cal Abrams, who had also received death threats because he was Jewish, crossed home plate after a home run and waited for Jackie to do the same. Then he took Jackie's arm and walked back to the dugout, saying, "If they are ever gonna shoot the two of us, now's the time." But there were no shots and no more incidents that year.

Jackie battled more than anonymous threats in 1950. During spring training, he had injured his ankle. He'd decided to play anyway, even though he couldn't run very well. Then he collided with a catcher and hurt his left knee so badly he could hardly bend it. He spent a few days on the bench, then pulled a muscle in his left thigh. He kept playing, but was then hit in the elbow by a pitch. The elbow swelled, and he had to sit out again. In September he jammed his thumb and tore some tendons in his left hand. "Whatever happened to me in 1950 happened on my left side," he said. Despite these injuries, his batting average in 1950 was .328, with 14 home runs, 99 runs scored, and 81 runs batted in. He was also the best second baseman in the National League, with a fielding average of .986. He set a league record for double plays with 153 and was chosen again for the National League All-Star team.

Even with Jackie's personal success that year, the Dodgers didn't win another pennant, and even worse,

Branch Rickey was leaving the organization. At the end of the season, Walter O'Malley, who disliked Rickey, replaced him. As president, O'Malley reportedly fined any Dodger a dollar for speaking Rickey's name. Jackie was disappointed at his friend's departure. He felt he owed Rickey his loyalty for giving him his chance in the big leagues and supporting him through the tough times. He was generally unhappy with O'Malley, who Jackie felt was not as supportive as he should have been. But Jackie got along well with the new manager, Chuck Dressen, and the two became good friends. O'Malley and Jackie never hit it off, and in a few seasons the dislike between the two, combined with other factors, would make Jackie happy to retire from baseball.

In 1951, however, retirement was far from his mind. The Dodgers fought their rivals the New York Giants for first place all season. On the last day of the season the Giants beat the Boston Braves to be in the championship game. The same day the Dodgers played the Philadelphia Phillies, with the winner of that game advancing to play a three-game championship series with the Giants.

In the eighth inning, the Dodgers managed to tie the score with the Phillies, 8-8. The game went into extra innings. In the 12th, with a Phillie on third base and two outs, the batter hit a ball to second base. It looked like the Phillies would win, and fans held their breath while Jackie Robinson dove to catch the ball. He slammed hard into the ground, jamming his elbow into his ribs, but when he finally rose, the ball was in his glove. He had saved the game for the Dodgers.

But the game was not over yet. In the 14th inning Jackie swung at a fastball and knocked it into the bleachers. The Dodgers won, 9-8. The stage was set for a three-game showdown with the Giants for the National League pennant.

The teams split the first two games of the series. In the deciding game Jackie scored first, and in the ninth inning the Dodgers led, 4-2. Unfortunately for the Dodgers and their fans, Bobby Thomson, with two outs and two runners on base, hit a home run. Radio announcer Russ Hodges chanted excitedly, "The Giants win the pennant! The Giants win the pennant! The Giants win the pennant!" while fans went wild over the upset. It was the legendary "shot heard 'round the world."

Jackie, alone among the Dodgers, went out of his way to congratulate the Giants' manager, Leo Durocher. His gesture was all the more remarkable for the well-known shouting matches he and Durocher engaged in on the diamond. Durocher later remarked of the incident, "Jackie Robinson had class. He was some man."

During the 1952 season Jackie and Rae's second son, David, was born. Jackie's troubles off the field continued despite the happy event—it seemed he was constantly being quoted as saying something inflammatory or cited for doing something outrageous. Jackie simply stood up for his teammates against bad calls or unfair opponents, or else he stood up for his own right to equality. Even when his teammates also protested, Jackie got the publicity.

His problems with Dodger management continued. O'Malley called Jackie to his office in early 1952. He seemed to insinuate that Jackie's sore arm was not serious enough to warrant his not playing in exhibition games. He also wondered why Jackie protested his segregated living arrangements. He succeeded in infuriating not only Jackie, but Rae too. After that the working relationship between Jackie and O'Malley suffered.

A series of newspaper articles detailed Jackie's supposed quarrel with his teammate Roy Campanella. Newspapers insisted on comparing the two men, who had noticeably different personalities and different attitudes toward their roles as black citizens in a white society. Campy, for example, was reserved and shy. He shunned confrontation generally, saying, "I'm no crusader." Jackie, as his career attests, did not hesitate to speak up against racial prejudice wherever and whenever he encountered it. Despite their differences, Jackie respected Campy greatly and denied ever having a personal problem with his teammate. Nevertheless, unfavorable press followed him and made the 1952 season something less than memorable.

Matters did not improve when, early in 1953, Jackie appeared on a television show called *Youth Wants to Know*. During the program he was asked by one young lady if he thought the Yankees were prejudiced against African Americans. Jackie, as always, was blunt—he felt the Yankee players were "good guys," but the Yankee management had so far not signed a single black player. He didn't know his reply would spark a firestorm of protest, mostly from people who thought Jackie had used the show as a soapbox for preaching. But Jackie felt he had a responsibility to be honest and face the reality of racial discrimination.

The problem was a very real one for him. Despite Jackie's fame and salary, the Robinsons encountered housing discrimination. In 1952, after the birth of their third child, David, the Robinsons sought to move from their St. Albans, Long Island, home. Fans too often felt free to knock on the door at all hours, insisting on taking pictures of the Robinsons or getting autographs at inconvenient times. (Jackie's refusal to comply resulted in more bad press about his "attitude.") Jackie and Rae hoped to find a home in the country that would afford them more privacy as well as play areas for the children. They hoped they could find one in an integrated neighborhood. But when they found suitable homes and made offers, the houses were suddenly taken off the market or the selling prices had suddenly increased.

After two years of such frustrating unfairness, a newspaper journalist in Connecticut printed an article about the Robinsons' difficulties. Community and church leaders in Stamford, Connecticut, decided to form a committee to help. In 1955, when David was three years old, the Robinsons were finally able to move into their new home, which

they had planned and built themselves. The house was in an all-white neighborhood, and at the nearest public school the Robinson children were the only African Americans. Jackie later wrote that this situation, combined with his celebrity status, made childhood difficult for the younger Robinsons.

Meanwhile, despite the prejudice the family faced, Jackie continued to shine for the Dodgers. Jackie was 34 in 1953, and his hair was turning gray. The years of playing sports and the injuries were beginning to take their toll. So, too, was the diabetes he had developed, which he never revealed to his teammates or manager. But he was still a good athlete and excited fans with his performance on the diamond.

His 1953 stats showed he still had the talent. His batting average was .329, up from the previous year's .308. He hit 12 home runs, scored 109 runs, and batted in another 95.

Ebbets Field bustled during the days of the Brooklyn Dodgers. Fans were devastated when just two years removed from winning the World Series their team was packed up and moved out west.

The Dodgers won the National League pennant that year, although they lost the World Series to the Yankees. The following season, Jackie still hit .311 with 15 home runs, although his other stats dropped off a bit: he scored just 62 runs and batted in 59.

In 1954 a new manager, Walter Alston, succeeded Chuck Dressen. Robinson thought Alston was a "quiet and decent" man, but "some of us on the team felt he lacked confidence and. . . was given to making some very unwise decisions and judgments in the heat of play." During the season, Jackie got angry at an umpire's call, and Alston did not back him up. Robinson snapped to a teammate that Alston had stood at third base "like a wooden Indian. . . . Here's a play that meant a run in a tight ball game, so whether I was right or wrong, the play was close enough for him to protest to the umpire. But not Alston. What kind of manager is that?" Jackie's relationship with Alston became even more tense after these comments.

In 1955 rumors circulated that the team felt it was time to replace Jackie. "Alston had me in the lineup one day and the next day on the bench," he said. "This is the way a ballplayer loses his timing and becomes rusty." Worse, Jackie and Alston got into a hot argument, and Jackie credited Gil Hodges with preventing him from taking a swing at Alston. "Take it easy, Jackie," Hodges said. "It's something not worth fighting about. Take it out on the other teams."

The whole team took the advice to heart, it seemed. The Dodgers led the National League in stolen bases, home runs, runs scored, batting average, and slugging percentage during the 1955 season. In addition, their pitching staff finished the season with the most saves and strikeouts in the league, along with the lowest earned run average (ERA). The Dodgers finished $13^1/_2$ games ahead of second-place Milwaukee.

Yet another World Series meeting with the Yankees awaited. Despite having missed a third of the season with

Jackie is congratulated after crossing the plate in World Series action against the Yankees. A Dodger uniform was the only one in the majors Jackie would ever wear.

injuries, Jackie couldn't wait for another crack at the Yanks.

On September 28 the Series got under way. The Dodgers trailed 6-4 in the top of the eighth when Jackie reached third base. With one out, pitcher Whitey Ford focused on retiring the next batter. On the first pitch, Jackie noticed that neither the pitcher nor the catcher was paying him any attention. There was little reason they should.

With less than two outs and his team down by two runs, conventional baseball wisdom was that a base runner on third base shouldn't take chances. After all, the base runner could score not only on a base hit but also on a sacrifice fly or a groundout to the right side of the infield. But the daring Jackie Robinson wasn't interested in conventional baseball wisdom.

As Ford went into his windup for the next pitch, Jackie darted for home. He was trying to accomplish baseball's most difficult baserunning feat: stealing home, literally racing the ball to the plate. Jackie barreled toward the plate. His slide caused catcher Yogi Berra to miss the tag. Jackie had stolen home.

Despite his amazing steal of home, the Dodgers lost the first game, 6-5. The Yankees took the second game as well. Heading back to Ebbetts Field, the Dodgers were in a 2-0 hole.

In the third game, the mere threat of Jackie's baserunning helped him give his team an early 3-2 lead. After singling, his presence on the base paths caused the Yankees' pitcher to hit the next batter with a pitch, give up a bunt single, and walk the next batter, allowing Jackie to score.

In the later innings, with the Dodgers leading 6-3, Jackie slapped a Tom Surdivant pitch off the left-field wall. A wide turn around second was followed by a fake back to the bag. When the outfielder threw behind him to second, Jackie took third. He later scored on a base hit, and the Dodgers won, 8-3.

"He comes to beat you," Durocher said of Jackie's baserunning. "He comes to win."

The teams eventually squared off in a deciding seventh game. To the delight of Brooklyn, the Dodgers took the game and the Series. The Dodgers were world champions! "THIS IS NEXT YEAR!" jubilant newspaper headlines proclaimed.

Overall, Jackie's play was not the greatest in the 1955 World Series—he batted his lowest Series average, .182, with 5 runs and one run batted in—but his brashness invigorated his team.

During the 1956 season Jackie was benched much of the time, but he managed to hit a respectable .275, score

61 runs, and bat in 43 more. He also hit eight home runs. At the end of the 1956 season, the Dodgers again won the National League pennant and faced the Yankees in the World Series. In one of the games, Yankee pitcher Don Larsen pitched the only perfect game in World Series history. Brooklyn fans were disappointed again when the Dodgers lost the Series.

This time, however, there would be only one more "next year." Beyond disappointment, Brooklyn fans were heartbroken when news broke in early 1957 that the Dodgers would move to Los Angeles at the end of that season.

When he felt it was time to leave baseball, Jackie wasn't looking back. He had a job lined up and wanted to contribute to the civil rights movement. He reportedly said he wouldn't play again for one million dollars, an unheard of salary at the time.

Jackie was always attentive to his family. Though he remained active in business, retirement from baseball enabled him to spend more time with his children.

Ebbets Field was famous for being an intimate stadium where fans sat very close to the field. Brooklyn fans were famous themselves for the number of bizarre characters among them. One woman named Hilda showed up in the front row at every home game with her own sign saying, "Hilda's Here!" and she rang cow bells when the Dodgers did well. Hilda regularly shouted advice to players, and, in the small stadium, it was clearly heard.

Another group of fans wore a rough uniform and played musical instruments fairly badly. They marched around the stands leading Brooklyn fans in cheers. Red Barber, a famous radio announcer, dubbed the marching band the Brooklyn Sym-Phony.

The Dodgers had been named in honor of the many streetcars in Brooklyn that forced pedestrians to take extra care dodging traffic. The team and Ebbets Field were always an integral part of life in the borough. Since the 1930s when the Dodgers played poorly, Brooklyn fans called the team "dem bums"—the spelling reflecting the accent of many of the borough's citizens. When the team began to do well and win pennants, the name stuck, but with more affection. Fans wore pins saying, "Our Bums!" and "Moider [as in murder] Dem Yanks!"

But history couldn't keep the Dodgers in Brooklyn. Ebbets Field was to be torn down. Then, in December, Jackie Robinson was traded to—of all teams—the New York Giants. It was the end of an era. Jackie, though, would never wear a Giants uniform—he had already decided to retire from baseball.

Jackie could have remained in organized baseball as a manager or even part of the front-office organization. However, no such offers were made, and he had sold the rights to his retirement story to *Look* magazine. He could not answer the announcement of his being traded until the magazine released the story. Controversy arose when the magazine hit the stands in January 1957. The Dodgers claimed that he was merely holding out for more money from the Giants. And the Giants did tell Jackie he could name his salary. He wrote that he was flattered the Giants believed in him, but he knew that his game was fading. "The Giants are a team that need youth and rebuilding. The team doesn't need me," he announced. Jackie felt his name and skills would be put to better use in the business world. Besides, leaving baseball meant he would not have to travel so much anymore and could spend time with his wife and growing children.

Jackie continued to be a popular figure in baseball circles regardless of his involvement in controversial political and social issues. He remained obliging to fans throughout his life.

7

THE LAST INNINGS

JACKIE ACCEPTED an executive position with the company Chock Full O' Nuts in 1956. The owner, William Black, was white, but he employed many African Americans. Black had started his business with one store and worked to build it into a large chain, selling his products in grocery stores and elsewhere. Jackie respected Black, and Black, in turn, gave him a real position in community relations, not just a title. Jackie spent the next several years tending to the needs of the company's black employees. He also worked to improve the company's reputation, particularly in black communities. Years later he remembered being told how people would come into stores selling Chock Full O' Nuts products and say, "Give me a can of that Jackie Robinson coffee."

While with the company Jackie was asked to chair a drive for the Freedom Fund of the National Association for the Advancement of Colored People (NAACP). In December 1956, the organization had awarded him the Springarn Medal, given annually to an African American outstanding in his or her field. His achievement in integrating major league baseball made him a symbol, and his out-spokenness in insisting on black equality had made him a leader in civil rights as well. Naturally, he was interested in helping the NAACP in the fight for civil rights, and William Black allowed him to keep his job while raising money for the NAACP.

He again refused to be a figurehead chairman. He went on a speaking tour, initially speaking for only a few min-utes at a time. As he grew more comfortable with the posi-tion, and more knowledgeable about the NAACP itself, he began to speak longer. With Jackie as its chairman, the Fund Drive accumulated one million dollars for the first time. He later teamed with other members of the staff to hold a benefit dinner that raised over $75,000.

In addition to his work at Chock Full O' Nuts, he was elected to the National Board of Directors of the NAACP, a post he held until he resigned in 1967. By that time Jackie felt that the organization had become too rigid and undemocratic. He believed that the NAACP needed to make room for younger and more progressive leadership. Despite his feelings, he continued for the rest of his life to work for civil rights and the improvement of the status of African Americans.

Jackie frequently took part in parades, political rallies, and demonstrations against inequality. The years before and after his retirement from baseball were very busy ones for the civil rights movement in America. Early in the 1950s Jackie had met Dr. Martin Luther King Jr., the civil rights leader who had organized bus boycotts across the South. The boycotts brought national attention to segrega-tion, and in 1956 the U.S. Supreme Court ruled segregation on public transportation illegal. King told Jackie he could never have accomplished what he had without the example Jackie had set in integrating baseball. Jackie forced him-self to follow a nonviolent approach to abuse during his first few years with the Dodgers; this was also the path taken by Dr. King during the 1950s in the bus boycotts,

lunch-counter sit-ins, and other demonstrations. (A sit-in was held when African Americans integrated restaurants and other segregated facilities by sitting in them for as long as it took to be served. Often their nonviolent actions got them arrested and jailed.) The two men deeply respected each other's views, even when they disagreed on subjects like U.S. involvement in Vietnam. Both Jackie and King received honorary degrees from Harvard University.

Jackie also organized concerts at his home in Stamford. Black students arrested and jailed for a sit-in in North Carolina appealed to Jackie Robinson for help in 1960. His response was to organize a benefit concert. Ella Fitzgerald, Duke Ellington, Sarah Vaughn, Carmen McRae, and other African-American stars lent their talents

Martin Luther King Jr. (left) called on Jackie to drum up support for the civil rights movement. Jackie also offered opinions on presidential candidates.

Jackie was inducted into the Hall of Fame in 1962. His talent alone merited his induction in his first year of eligibility. The pressure he endured throughout his career only made him more worthy of the honor.

to Jackie's "An Afternoon of Jazz" to raise more than $20,000. The "Afternoon of Jazz" became an annual event, and in later years, Jackie Jr. helped organize it.

Jackie kept busy in other ways after he retired from baseball. He wrote a regular column with his friend Alfred Duckett and used it to speak out on issues affecting African Americans and racial prejudice in general. Duckett, who was a speechwriter for Dr. King, later collaborated with Jackie on three books, including Jackie's 1972 autobiography, *I Never Had It Made.*

Jackie was also active in politics. During the 1960 presidential campaign, he supported the Republican candidate, Richard Nixon, over the Democrat, John F. Kennedy. Jackie took the time and effort to meet each candidate. He wasn't overwhelmed by Vice President Nixon's record on civil rights matters. Nevertheless, Jackie felt his meeting with Senator Kennedy did not bode well for African Americans. Kennedy freely admitted he knew nothing about the black community, and his tendency not to look Jackie in the eye was disturbing.

As events unfolded, Kennedy was elected and the Democratic administration oversaw some of the greatest civil rights advancements in American history. Nixon, elected in 1968, resigned in 1973 to avoid impeachment for illegal activities.

Jackie received a great deal of criticism at the time and later for his support of Nixon, since most African Americans supported Kennedy. Jackie said later, "I do not consider my decision to back Richard Nixon . . . one of my finer ones. It was a sincere one, however, at the time."

Jackie had become such a figure of controversy in the press by the early 1960s that he was genuinely surprised to have been chosen for induction to the Baseball Hall of Fame. On July 23, 1962, he became the first African American so honored. A crowd of 5,000 watched as he received his plaque. In his speech he asked the three most important people in his life to step forward and share the accolades for his achievement in integrating baseball. His mother, Mallie, his wife, Rae, and Branch Rickey joined him before the crowd. Rickey's support of Jackie over the years had ripened into friendship, and before Jackie even retired from baseball, he felt that Rickey was like a father to him. He was deeply saddened by Rickey's death three years later.

In 1964 Jackie helped raise over one million dollars to found the Freedom National Bank. The bank was one of the only black-owned lending institutions at the time, and was concerned primarily with fairness to minorities in extending loans and credit. The bank's mission was in keeping with Jackie's belief that black Americans use the power of "the ballot and the buck" to change their lives. The organized economic and political power of the black community, Jackie believed, could change society. With his help the bank became one of the largest black-owned banks in the United States.

Also in 1964 Jackie left his position with Chock Full O' Nuts to work with New York governor Nelson Rockefeller. Jackie was one of Rockefeller's six deputy national directors in his campaign for the Republican nomination for president. "I was not as sold on the Republican party as I was on the governor," Jackie wrote. "Every chance I got, while I was campaigning, I said plainly what I thought of the right-wing Republicans and the harm they were doing." He was upset when one of these right-wingers, Barry Goldwater, won the Republican nomination. But Jackie continued to support Rockefeller, and in 1966 became the governor's special assistant for community affairs.

When Richard Nixon and Spiro Agnew became the Republican nominees for president and vice president in 1968, Jackie resigned his post rather than embarrass Rockefeller by supporting Democrat Hubert Humphrey. Of his time in Rockefeller's administration, Jackie said, "I did what I could. . . . I felt the job was worthwhile and that I had made some progress for the black cause while I was in it."

On April 4, 1968, Martin Luther King Jr. was shot and killed in Memphis, Tennessee. In June Robert Kennedy, who many believe was the force behind his brother's presidential efforts for civil rights, was shot in Los Angeles. The riots in many urban areas, the intensification of the Vietnam War, and other shattering events made the year a difficult one for many Americans.

It was also a hard year for Jackie—and not simply because of the civil unrest, his disillusionment with the

Republican Party, or some serious problems with the Freedom National Bank. His health suffered that year, as his legs and particularly an old knee problem worsened. Doctors did not make the connection between his problems walking and his diabetes. In 1968 Jackie's mother, Mallie, passed away at her home in Pasadena. To make matters even worse, his relationship with his older son, Jackie Jr., had been tense for some time.

Jackie Jr. had problems in school and eventually dropped out. The Robinsons were always loving and supportive parents, but as the boy grew up, Jackie and his son found it difficult to communicate. Once Jackie Jr. ran away from home and hitchhiked to California, hoping to find

Jackie and Rae Robinson (center) host "An Afternoon of Jazz" at their Stamford, Connecticut, home. Jackie organized the annual concerts to benefit the NAACP.

himself by traveling and working. In 1964, at age 17, he decided to enlist in the army in the hope of straightening out his confused life. Within a year he was sent into combat in Vietnam. There he faced the hell that all American soldiers experienced, and he was seriously wounded. His father remarked, "One of his best buddies was killed and another died in his arms. This happened as Jackie was trying to drag his own wounded body back behind the lines." In June 1967 Jackie Jr. was discharged from the army.

But Jackie Jr. had experienced more than combat in Vietnam. He came home with a drug addiction. After some brushes with the law and several attempts at rehabilitation in a hospital, Jackie Jr. was not improving. He was involved in criminal activities to support his habit. When he was arrested and given a choice between prison or a rehabilitation program, he enrolled in a program called Daytop in Seymour, Connecticut. For three years Jackie Jr. immersed himself in overcoming his addiction and straightening out his life. Always close, the Robinson family had supported their son and brother throughout his troubles. Grateful to the program that had helped him recover, the Robinsons held a picnic for the Daytop center at their home in Stamford. Jackie later wrote:

> [O]n the evening of the picnic, our confused and lost kid who had gone off to war, who had experienced as much life in a few short and turbulent years as many never do in a lifetime, that same kid had now become a young man, growing in self-esteem, growing in confidence. . . . I stuck out my hand to shake his hand, remembering the day of his departure for the service [when Jackie Jr. had refused a hug]. He brushed my hand aside, pulled me to him, and embraced me in a tight hug.
>
> That single moment paid for every bit of sacrifice, every bit of anguish, I had ever undergone. I had my son back.

In late 1970 Jackie Jr. testified before a U.S. Senate subcommittee about his drug problem, which began during his military service. In 1971 Jackie Jr. took a job on the staff of the Daytop center and, to express his gratitude to the program, began arranging "An Afternoon of Jazz" to benefit Daytop. Tragically, only days before the concert in June 1971, Jackie Jr. was killed in a car accident. The Robinsons were devastated. But his family was aware of the importance the concert had held for Jackie Jr., and the benefit was held six days after his funeral.

By 1971 Jackie's health had deteriorated, too. Though he was still a relatively young man at 52, diabetes had ravaged his once athletic physique, weakening the blood vessels in his body. Even before he retired from baseball in 1957, Jackie had suffered serious problems. One friend remembered the day in the early 1950s when Jackie learned he was diabetic: "[T]he doctor told him that for a person who had competed in athletics for as long as [Jackie] had, he had never seen a body that was as deteriorated." Still, none of Jackie's teammates ever knew of his condition.

Jackie's busy life and serious stresses in the 1960s contributed to his early decline. He had survived two heart attacks, in 1962 and 1965, and suffered from high blood pressure. He was sometimes unable to get out of bed. Blood vessels in Jackie's legs and behind his eyes burst, causing him to walk with a limp and lose all vision in one eye as well as most of his vision in the other.

Jackie was still very much a public figure, even an idol. When Jackie learned he might go completely blind, he was deeply moved by the following telegram, from a black woman in Detroit, printed in the *New York Times*:

I AM TRYING TO GET IN TOUCH WITH JACKIE ROBINSON THAT ONCE PLAYED WITH THE BROOKLYN DODGERS. WILL YOU PLEASE PRINT THIS AND WHATEVER IT COSTS SEND ME THE BILL AND ILL PAY YOU. "JACKIE I READ IN THE FREE PRESS THIS MORNING THAT YOU'VE LOST SIGHT IN YOUR RIGHT EYE AND IS VERY BAD IN THE LEFT. DO YOU THINK A TRANSPLANT WILL

Old teammates like Roy Campanella (in wheelchair) and Pee Wee Reese (pall-bearer on right) turned out to pay their last respects to Jackie, a strong indication that he lived up to the words that became his epitaph (opposite page).

HELP. I WILL BE GLAD TO GIVE YOU ONE OF MINE. YOU CAN CALL ME AT WORK BETWEEN 8:15 AND 5:30 PM."

Despite his deteriorating health, Jackie made several public appearances. In April 1972 Jackie and Rae attended the funeral of Jackie's teammate and friend Gil Hodges. There Jackie apologized to his old friend Pee Wee Reese for his inability to recognize him. In June Jackie and Rae were honored at a ceremony in Los Angeles to retire his number, 42. He made a speech commemorating the 25th anniversary of the integration of baseball. Fans were surprised at his old, tired appearance—his weight gain, his white hair, and his limp.

On October 15 Jackie was present to toss out the first ball at the second game of the World Series in Cincinnati. Just before the ceremony, he chatted with his former teammates Pee Wee Reese and Joe Black. Reese asked about his vision, and Jackie replied, "The left eye just floods with blood, the right eye I can see images. But that's not the main thing. I'm gonna go into the hospital and have my leg amputated."

Jackie spoke "like he was talking about apples and oranges," Joe Black remembered. Reese was understandably shocked. Jackie reassured him, "I'll . . . get an artificial leg and I'll learn to walk and I'll play golf, and you know what, Pee Wee? . . . I'll still beatcha."

When he was called to the microphone, Jackie aroused controversy yet again by declaring that he was pleased to be there that day, "but I will be more pleased the day I can look over at the third-base line and see a black man as manager."

Jackie never lived to see that day, which came only a year later. On October 24, 1972, Jackie Robinson died at home of a heart attack. Nearly 3,000 people attended his funeral in New York.

Rev. Jesse Jackson, a longtime friend, delivered the eulogy, comparing Jackie's lifework to a chess game. "He was the black knight and he checkmated bigotry," Jackson declared. The dates on his gravestone, 1919 to 1972, would be separated by a dash, Jackson said. "On that dash, he snapped the barbed wire of prejudice . . . in his last dash, Jackie stole home and Jackie is safe."

Pallbearers for Jackie's casket included his teammates Pee Wee Reese, Don Newcombe, and Ralph Branca and basketball great Bill Russell. Many other public figures attended, including Chicago Cubs player Ernie Banks, home run king Hank Aaron, and former teammate Carl Erskine. A hero of Jackie's childhood, Joe Louis, was also there. "Jackie is my hero," Louis said later. "He don't bite his tongue for nothing. I just don't have the guts, you might call it, to say what he says." Roy Campanella, who was paralyzed in a car accident in 1958, also attended Jackie's funeral.

In 1986 President Reagan, whom Jackie had once described as someone he "could never be associated with" politically, awarded the Presidential Medal of Freedom to Jackie Robinson. It is the highest civilian award in the United States, given only to those who have contributed significantly to the advancement of American ideals. His legacy is seen in the fact that 40 percent of major league players are currently African American.

In 1997 baseball commemorated the 50th anniversary of his entrance into the majors by retiring his number 42. No player who did not already have that as his jersey number at the time will ever wear the number again.

Though there is still work to be done, with only 3 teams out of 28 having black managers, Jackie's impact on race relations is undeniable. Roger Wilkins, a distinguished civil rights activist, remarked, "Jackie forced people, all people, to reconsider their assumptions about race."

"Through baseball," Jackie's colleague Don Newcombe said, "Jackie did more to tear down segregation in hotels and sports arenas than any other man. Nobody will ever do more, because it won't be necessary again."

On and off the field, Jackie Robinson was a pioneer of civil rights. He worked and played tirelessly, at great risk to his health and even his life. Many, including Pee Wee Reese, believe that his life was shortened by the adversity he faced—and conquered. He overcame racism, personal tragedy, desperate poverty, physical injuries, and ill health to become one of the greatest players in baseball. More significant, he was also one of the most important Americans of the 20th century, as an activist, a hero, and a role model for millions.

CHRONOLOGY

1919   Jack Roosevelt Robinson born near Cairo, Georgia, January 31

1920   Mallie Robinson and her five children move to Pasadena, CA

1937   Jackie enrolls at Pasadena Junior College

1939   Brother Frank is killed in motorcycle accident; Jackie enrolls at UCLA

1941   Leaves UCLA before graduation to work; plays for Honolulu Bears, an integrated minor-league football team

1942   Drafted into U.S. Army

1944   Court-martialed, cleared of charges and receives honorable discharge

1945   Joins Kansas City Monarchs (Negro leagues baseball team); meets Branch Rickey in August and signs contract with the Montreal Royals in October

1946   Marries Rachel (Rae) Isum in February; plays for Montreal Royals; team wins Little World Series; son Jackie Jr. born in November

1947   Becomes first African American to play in major leagues (Brooklyn Dodgers) in 20th century, April 15; voted National League Rookie of the Year and leads league in stolen bases

1949   Testifies before HUAC in July; is voted National League's Most Valuable Player; leads league in batting average and stolen bases

1950   Daughter Sharon born in January; films *The Jackie Robinson Story* before baseball season; Robinson family moves to St. Albans (Long Island), NY; Branch Rickey leaves Dodgers for Pittsburgh

1952   Son David born in May

1955   Brooklyn Dodgers win their first World Series

1956   Receives prestigious Springarn Medal from NAACP; Dodgers announce move to Los Angeles

1957   Announces his retirement from baseball in January; takes job in community relations at Chock Full O' Nuts company; chairs NAACP Freedom Fund drive

1962   Inducted into Baseball Hall of Fame (the first year he is eligible)

1966   Becomes special assistant for community affairs to Governor Rockefeller

1968   Campaigns for Hubert Humphrey for president; Mallie Robinson dies

1969	Jackie Jr. returns wounded from Vietnam, enters drug rehabilitation program a few months later
1971	Jackie Jr. dies in car accident
1972	Number (42) is retired by the Dodgers; Jackie dies October 24
1986	Posthumously awarded the Presidential Medal of Freedom
1997	Major league baseball retires number 42 leaguewide

JACKIE ROBINSON'S STATISTICS

Year	Avg.	G	AB	R	H	2B	3B	HR	RBI	SO	OBP	SLG
1947	.297	151	590	125	175	31	5	12	48	36	.383	.427
1948	.296	147	574	108	170	38	8	12	85	37	.367	.453
1949	.342	156	593	122	203	38	12	16	124	27	.432	.528
1950	.328	144	518	99	170	39	4	14	81	24	.423	.500
1951	.338	153	548	106	185	33	7	19	88	27	.429	.527
1952	.308	149	510	104	157	17	3	19	75	40	.440	.465
1953	.329	136	484	109	159	34	7	12	95	30	.425	.502
1954	.311	124	386	62	120	22	4	15	59	20	.413	.505
1955	.256	105	317	51	81	6	2	8	36	18	.378	.363
1956	.275	117	357	61	98	15	2	10	43	32	.382	.412
Totals	.311	1,382	4877	947	1518	273	54	137	734	291	.409	.474

FURTHER READING

Allen, Maury. *Jackie Robinson: A Life Remembered.* New York and Toronto: Franklin Watts, 1987.

Candaele, Kerry. *Bound for Glory, 1910–1930: From the Great Migration to the Harlem Renaissance.* Philadelphia: Chelsea House, 1997.

Coombs, Karen Mueller. *Jackie Robinson: Baseball's Civil Rights Legend.* Springfield, NJ: Enslow Publishers, 1997.

Dingle, Derek. *First in the Field: Baseball Hero Jackie Robinson.* New York: Hyperion Books for Children, 1998.

Dornfeld, Margaret. *The Turning Tide, 1948–1956: From the Desegregation of the Armed Forces to the Montgomery Bus Boycott.* Philadelphia: Chelsea House, 1995.

Falkner, David. *Great Time Coming: The Life of Jackie Robinson from Baseball to Birmingham.* New York and London: Simon and Schuster, 1995.

Fremon, David. *The Negro Baseball Leagues.* New York: New Discovery Books, 1994.

Gilbert, Thomas. *Baseball at War: World War II and the Fall of the Color Line.* New York and London: Franklin Watts, 1997.

———. *Baseball and the Color Line.* New York and London: Franklin Watts, 1995.

Hine, Darlene Clark. *The Path to Equality, 1931–1947: From the Scottsboro Case to the Breaking of Baseball's Color Barrier.* Philadelphia: Chelsea House, 1995.

Jacobs, William Jay. *They Shaped the Game: Ty Cobb, Babe Ruth, Jackie Robinson.* New York: Charles Scribner's Sons, 1994.

Kahn, Roger. *The Boys of Summer.* New York: Harper and Row, 1972.

Moffi, Larry, and Jonathan Kronstadt. *Crossing the Line: Black Major Leaguers, 1947–1959.* Iowa City: University of Iowa Press, 1994.

O'Connor, Jim. *Jackie Robinson and the Story of All-Black Baseball.* New York: Random House, 1989.

Peterson, Robert. *Only the Ball Was White: A History of Legendary Black Players and All-Black Professional Teams.* New York and Oxford: Oxford University Press, 1970.

Rampersad, Arnold. *Jackie Robinson: A Biography.* New York: Alfred A. Knopf, 1997.

Riley, James. *The Negro Leagues.* Philadelphia: Chelsea House Publishers, 1997.

Robinson, Jackie (as told to Alfred Duckett). *I Never Had It Made: An Autobiography.* Hopewell, NJ: Ecco Press, 1995.

Robinson, Jackie, and Alfred Duckett. *Breakthrough to the Big League: The Story of Jackie Robinson.* Lakeville, CT: Grey Castle Press, 1965.

Robinson, Sharon. *Stealing Home.* New York: HarperCollins, 1996.

Santella, Andrew. *Jackie Robinson Breaks the Color Line.* New York and London: Franklin Watts, 1996.

Scott, Richard. *Jackie Robinson: Baseball Great.* New York and Philadelphia: Chelsea House, 1987.

Smith, Robert. *Pioneers of Baseball.* Boston and Toronto: Little, Brown and Co., 1978.

INDEX

Aaron, Hank, 92
Abrams, Cal, 69
"Afternoon of Jazz, An," 83-84, 88-89
Agnew, Spiro, 86
Alston, Walter, 74
Amoros, Sandy, 38
Anderson, Carl, 16-17
Argyle Hotel Athletics, 26
Army, U.S., 22-25, 68
    integration of, 55

Bankhead, Dan, 38, 61
Banks, Ernie, 92
Barber, Red, 78
Baseball color line. *See* color line, baseball.
Bell, James "Cool Papa," 28, 34
Berra, Yogi, 76
Black, Joe, 12, 38, 91
Black, William, 81, 82
"Black Sox" scandal, 27-28
Boston Braves, 52-53, 70
Boston Red Sox, 34, 58
Boys of Summer, The (Kahn), 11
Bragan, Bobby, 48
Branca, Ralph, 92
Brooklyn, New York, 47, 55, 65, 78-79
Brooklyn Dodgers, 11, 33, 37, 38, 47-55, 58, 59-79, 89
    move to Los Angeles, 77
Brooklyn Sym-Phony, 78
Brown, Willard, 57
"Brown Dodgers," 33, 34

Cairo, Georgia, 12

Campanella, Roy, 38, 61, 64, 65, 71, 92
Carpenter, Bob, 52
Casey, Hugh, 48
Chandler, Happy, 51, 62
Chapman, Ben, 51-52, 63
Chicago Cubs, 64, 92
Chicago White Sox, 27
Chock Full O' Nuts, 81, 82, 86
Cincinnati Reds, 27
Civil Rights Act, 55
Civil rights movement, 82-84, 85
Cleveland Indians, 57, 58
Color line, baseball, 12, 25-28, 33-37, 47-59, 90
Cuba, 47
Cuban Giants, 26-27

Daytop, 88, 89
Dee, Ruby, 68
Diabetes, 11, 73, 87
Doby, Larry, 57
Downs, Karl, 16-17, 25, 39, 55
Dressen, Chuck, 70, 74
Duckett, Alfred, 84
Durocher, Leo, 48, 50, 59, 71, 76

Eastern Colored League, 28
East-West Game, 33
Ellington, Duke, 83
Erskine, Carl, 11, 92

Federal Bureau of Investigation (FBI), 69
Fitzgerald, Ella, 83
Ford, Whitey, 75-76

Fort Hood, Texas, 24
Fort Riley, Kansas, 22, 24
Foster, Rube, 28, 58
Freedom Fund, 81
Freedom National Bank, 85-86, 87
Frick, Ford, 53
Furillo, Carl, 48

Galloway, Bill, 27
Gibson, Josh, 28, 34
Gilliam, Junior, 38
Goldwater, Barry, 86
Great Depression, 28

Harvard University, 83
Heart disease, 11, 17, 92
Hodges, Gil, 48, 74, 90
Hodges, Russ, 71
Homestead Grays, 28, 40
Honolulu Bears, 22
Hopper, Clay, 39, 41, 43
House Un-American Activities Committee (HUAC), 68
Humphrey, Hubert, 86

I Never Had It Made (Robinson), 14, 84
International League, 26, 40, 43, 44

Jackie Robinson Story, The (film), 68-69
Jackson, Jesse, 92
Jersey City Little Giants, 41-42
Jim Crow laws, 26, 38
John Muir Technical High School, 17

Jones, Sam, 64

Kahn, Roger, 11, 63
Kansas City Monarchs, 25, 28, 29-33, 35, 38, 57, 58-59
Kennedy, John F., 85
Kennedy, Robert, 86
King, Martin Luther, Jr., 82-83, 84, 86

Landis, Kenesaw Mountain, 27-28
Larsen, Don, 77
Little World Series, 43
Look magazine, 79
Louis, Joe, 14, 22, 92

McRae, Carmen, 83
Martin, Sam, 43
Montreal Royals, 37, 39-44, 47, 49

National Association for the Advancement of Colored People (NAACP), 81-82
National Association of Colored Professional Baseball Clubs, 28
National Youth Administration, 21
Negro American League, 28, 29, 58-59
Negro leagues, 25, 28-35, 38, 39, 58-59
Negro National League, 28, 39
Negro World Series, 28
Newark Eagles, 40

Newcombe, Don, 38, 61, 64, 92, 93
New York City, 11, 54
New York Giants, 57, 60, 70-71, 79
New York Times, 89
New York Yankees, 54, 64, 72, 74-77
Nixon, Richard, 85, 86

Officer Candidate School, 22
Olympics, 1936 Summer, 17
O'Malley, Walter, 70, 71-72
O'Neil, Buck, 30, 63
Owens, Jesse, 17

Paige, LeRoy "Satchel," 28, 30, 33, 34
Partlow, Roy, 61
Pasadena, California, 12, 35, 87
Pasadena Junior College, 17-18
Pepper Street Gang, 15-17
Peterson, Robert, 57, 59
Philadelphia Phillies, 50-52, 53, 70
Pittsburgh Courier, 58
Pittsburgh Crawfords, 40
Presidential Medal of Freedom, 92

Racism, 13-14, 15, 16, 21-25, 30-31, 39-40, 42-43, 44, 67-68, 71, 72-73, 92-93
    in baseball, 25-28, 33-35, 37-39, 50-55, 62-63, 69
Reagan, Ronald, 92
Reese, Pee Wee, 48, 53, 54,

60, 61, 90, 91, 92, 93
Rickey, Branch, 33-37, 38, 40, 47, 49, 52, 62, 70, 85
Riley, James, 27
Robeson, Paul, 68
Robinson, David (son), 71, 72
Robinson, Edgar (brother), 12
Robinson, Frank (brother), 12, 17, 18
Robinson, Frank, 58
Robinson, Jack Roosevelt "Jackie,"
    as All-Star, 64, 69
    in the army, 22-25, 30, 35, 68
    autobiography of, 14, 84
    awards of, 18, 44, 54, 64, 81-82, 83, 92
    and baseball color line, 11, 47-55, 90
    and Baseball Hall of Fame, 85
    and basketball, 17, 18, 19, 21, 25
    birth of, 12
    childhood of, 12-17
    and Chock Full O' Nuts, 81, 82, 86
    and civil rights movement, 82-84, 85
    as coach, 21, 25, 61
    in college athletics, 17-19, 35
    court-martialed, 25
    as critic of racism, 12, 14, 22-25, 30, 34-37, 51, 62-63, 67-68, 71, 72, 91, 92-93

death of, 92
education of, 17, 18
and football, 17-18, 19, 21-22
and Freedom National Bank, 85-86, 87
health problems of, 11, 43, 54, 73, 87, 89-90, 91, 93
and House Un-American Activities Committee (HUAC), 68
injuries of, 17, 18, 60, 64, 69, 73, 93
major league career, 47-79
marriage of, 25, 37, 39
minor league career, 37-44
and Most Valuable Player Award, 64
as movie actor, 68-69
and NAACP, 81-82
Negro league career, 25, 29-35
and politics, 85, 86
and racism, 13-14, 15, 16, 21-25, 30-31, 39-40, 42-43, 44, 50-55, 62-63, 67-68, 69, 71, 72-73, 92-93
and Branch Rickey, 35-37, 40, 49, 70, 85
and Springarn Medal, 81-82
and track and field, 17, 18, 19

traded to New York Giants, 79
World Series appearances, 54, 64, 74-77
Robinson, Jack Roosevelt, Jr. (son), 44, 47, 54-55, 65, 68, 84, 87-89
Robinson, Jerry (father), 12
Robinson, Mack (brother), 12, 15, 17, 18
Robinson, Mallie (mother), 12, 14, 15, 16, 18, 19, 31, 37, 85, 87
Robinson, Rachel "Rae" Isum (wife), 19, 25, 31, 37, 39-40, 44, 47, 49, 54-55, 65, 68, 72, 79, 85, 90
Robinson, Sharon (daughter), 65, 68
Robinson, Willa Mae (sister), 12, 14, 17
Rochelli, Lou, 40-41
Rockefeller, Nelson, 86
Russell, Bill, 92

St. Albans, New York, 72
St. Louis Browns, 57
St. Louis Cardinals, 53
Sam Houston College, 25
Scott, Richard, 64
761st Tank Battalion, 24
Sharecropping, 12
Shotton, Burt, 50, 60
Slaughter, Enos, 53
Smith, Wendell, 34, 58
Snider, Duke, 63-64
Sporting News, 54

Springarn Medal, 81
Stamford, Connecticut, 72, 83, 88
Stanky, Eddie, 48, 51
Sukeforth, Clyde, 33, 34, 35, 40
Surdivant, Tom, 76

Texas, 12, 24, 25, 55
Thompson, Henry, 57
Thomson, Bobby, 71

United States League, 33
University of California at Los Angeles (UCLA), 18-19, 21, 35

Vaughn, Sarah, 83
Veeck, Bill, 57
Vietnam War, 83, 86, 88

Walker, Dixie, 38, 48
Wilkins, Roger, 92-93
World Series
    1919, 27-28
    1947, 54
    1949, 64
    1953, 74
    1955, 74-77
    1956, 77
    1972, 91
World War II, 21, 22
Wright, John, 40

YMCA, 14, 61
Youth Wants to Know (television show), 72

PICTURE CREDITS

GINA DE ANGELIS is the author of *The Black Cowboys, Morgan Freeman, Gregory Hines,* and several other nonfiction books for young people. She holds a master's degree in history and lives in Williamsburg, VA.

JAMES SCOTT BRADY serves on the board of trustees with the Center to Prevent Handgun Violence and is the vice chairman of the Brain Injury Foundation. Mr. Brady served as assistant to the president and White House press secretary under President Ronald Reagan. He was severely injured in an assassination attempt on the president, but remained the White House press secretary until the end of the administration. Since leaving the White House, Mr. Brady has lobbied for stronger gun laws. In November 1993, President Bill Clinton signed the Brady Bill, a national law requiring a waiting period on handgun purchases and a background check on buyers.